EUROPEAN JOURNAL OF DEVELOPMENTAL PSYCHOLOGY
2011, 8 (1), 1–4

National identity and in-group/out-group attitudes in children: The role of sociohistorical settings. An introduction to the special issue

Louis Oppenheimer[1] and Martyn Barrett[2]

[1]Department of Developmental Psychology, University of Amsterdam, Amsterdam, The Netherlands
[2]Department of Psychology, University of Surrey, Guildford, Surrey, UK

In this short introduction, the background, rationale, and hypotheses are presented for the studies that are reported in the special issue, as well as the order in which the studies are presented.

Keywords: National identity; In-group/out-group attitudes; Sociohistorical settings.

The purpose of this special issue is to report on the findings of a series of studies that examined national identity and in-group/out-group attitudes in 7- and 11-year-old children from countries that have not experienced violence or war in the recent past (England and The Netherlands) and countries that have recently been or still are subject to armed conflict or intergroup violence (Bosnia, northern and southern Cyprus, Northern Ireland, the Basque Country and Israel). In total, 12 national groups participated in these studies involving Bosnian and Serbian children (Bosnia), Greek Cypriot and Turkish Cypriot children (Cyprus), Catholic and Protestant children (Northern Ireland), Basque and Spanish children (the Basque Country), Jewish and Arab children (Israel), and Dutch and English children (The Netherlands and England).

The guiding hypothesis for these studies proposed that children's national identifications: (a) are related to the everyday patterns of discourse and

Correspondence should be addressed to Louis Oppenheimer, Department of Psychology, University of Amsterdam, Roetersstraat 15, 1018 WB Amsterdam. The Netherlands. E-mail: l.j.t.oppenheimer@uva.nl

© 2011 Psychology Press, an imprint of the Taylor & Francis Group, an Informa business
http://www.psypress.com/edp   DOI: 10.1080/17405629.2010.533948

practices that occur within the particular sociohistorical settings in which they are living; (b) are dynamic psychological constructs whose salience is context dependent; and (c) are part of a larger system of interacting multiple identifications (e.g., religious, gender, etc.). As a consequence, differences in the structure and content of national identity between age groups (i.e., 7- and 11-year-olds), as well as between children from different national groups (i.e., sociohistorical settings) may not only be the result of processes of knowledge acquisition and cognitive development but also of cohort and context effects, individual and/or gender differences, and the result of different identifications interacting with each other. Hence, in the following papers, the findings within each national group as well as between groups are analysed and discussed by age and gender patterns in terms of the cultural heritage of the particular group to which the children belong, the meanings that are associated with being a member of that group, and the precise pattern of historical and contemporary relationships that exist between their own group and the various out-groups towards which their attitudes were assessed.

In examining the relationship between national identification and attitudes towards the in-group and out-groups, we expected that:

1. When the national in-group is made salient, children will tend to rate the in-group more positively than out-groups. A number of studies have now reported that, from the age of 5, children make a distinction between the in-group and out-groups and typically (although not always) display a more positive attitude toward the in-group (e.g., Barrett, 2007; Bennett, Lyons, Sani, & Barrett, 1998; Bigler, Brown, & Markell, 2001; Bigler, Jones, & Lobliner, 1997; Masangkay, Villorente, Somcio, Reyes, & Taylor, 1972; Nesdale & Flesser, 2001; Poppe & Linssen, 1999; Teichman, 2001).
2. However, in line with the findings of recent analyses (Barrett, 2007; Bennett et al., 2004), it was anticipated that different patterns in the development of national identity and in-group/out-group attitudes would be exhibited in different sociohistorical settings.
3. Different sociohistorical settings were also expected to differentially affect the relationships between national identity and in-group/out-group attitudes (Barrett, 2007). Recent data (Oppenheimer, in press) suggest that such differences may also be affected by gender and age.

In this special issue, the findings of the studies conducted in England, Bosnia, Northern Ireland, northern Cyprus, southern Cyprus and the Basque Country are reported both separately and together as a cross-national comparative study, while the full comparative study addition- ally includes the data that were collected in The Netherlands and Israel.

Aims and scope

The *European Journal of Developmental Psychology* is an official publication of the European Society for Developmental Psychology. It publishes innovative original theoretical, empirical, methodological and review papers dealing with psychological development and developmental psychopathology during infancy, childhood and adolescence. It also publishes papers on social policy, based on developmental science and which are relevant to education, health or well-being in infancy, childhood and adolescence. It is keen to receive papers that are relevant to European developmental psychology in that they take account of topics such as European history, European policy or cultural diversity and their relevance to developmental matters. The Journal aims to cover the areas of cognitive and social development and the development of the person (self, identity and personality) and to do so from a disciplinary and/or an interdisciplinary perspective. On occasions, issues will be devoted to a special theme, under the editorship of an invited expert.

All subscription orders should be addressed to Psychology Press, c/o T&F Customer Services, Informa UK Ltd, Sheepen Place, Colchester, Essex, CO3 3LP, UK; Tel: +44 (0)20 7017 5544; Fax: +44 (0)20 7017 5198; E-mail: tf.enquiries@tfinforma.com. Send notices of change of address to the offices of the publishers at least six weeks in advance. Please include both old and new addresses.

Subscription rates for Volume 8, 2011 (6 issues)

To institutions (full subscription):	£401.00 (UK)	€533.00 (Europe)	$668.00 (Rest of World).
To institutions (online only):	£361.00 (UK)	€480.00 (Europe)	$601.00 (Rest of World).
To individuals:	£189.00 (UK)	€249.00 (Europe)	$310.00 (Rest of World).

An institutional subscription to the print edition also includes free access to the online edition for any number of concurrent users across a local area network.

Dollar rate applies to all subscribers outside Europe. Euro rates apply to all subscribers in Europe, except the UK and the Republic of Ireland where the pound sterling rate applies. All subscriptions are payable in advance and all rates include postage. Journals are sent by air to the USA, Canada, Mexico, India, Japan and Australasia. Subscriptions are entered on an annual basis, i.e., January to December. Payment may be made by sterling cheque, dollar cheque, euro cheque, international money order, National Giro or credit cards (Amex, Visa, and Mastercard).

Subscriptions purchased at the personal (print only) rate are strictly for personal, non-commercial use only. The reselling of personal subscriptions is strictly prohibited. Personal subscriptions must be purchased with a personal cheque or credit card. Proof of personal status may be requested. For full information please visit the Journal's homepage.

The *European Journal of Developmental Psychology* (USPS 022251) is published six times a year (in January, March, May, July, September, and November), by Psychology Press, 27 Church Road, Hove, BN3 2FA, UK. The 2011 US Institutional subscription price is $668.00. Airfreight and mailing in the USA by Agent named Air Business, C/O Worldnet Shipping USA Inc., 155-11 146th Avenue, Jamaica, New York, NY 11434, USA. **US Postmaster:** Send address changes to *European Journal of Developmental Psychology* (PEDP), Air Business Ltd, C/O Worldnet Shipping USA Inc., 155-11 146th Avenue, Jamaica, New York, NY 11434, USA.

Manuscripts are invited for submission: Please e-mail your paper, saved in a standard document format type such as Word or PDF, to **reviews@psypress.co.uk**. You may also contact the Editorial Assistant by phone on (0)2070 177730.

The journal's preferred maximum word limit is 5000 words in length. Abstracts should not exceed the number of 150 words. The space for References, Tables and Figures will be limited by the criterion of functionality.

Your covering e-mail/letter must include full contact details (including e-mail), the title of the journal to which you are submitting, and the title of your article.

All manuscripts must be accompanied by a statement confirming that it has not been previously published elsewhere and that it has not been submitted simultaneously for publication elsewhere.

All manuscripts should be submitted in American Psychological Association (APA) format following the latest edition of Publication Manual of the APA (currently 6th edition).

Copyright: It is a condition of publication that authors assign copyright or license the publication rights in their articles, including abstracts, to Taylor & Francis. This enables us to ensure full copyright protection and to disseminate the article, and of course the Journal, to the widest possible readership in print and electronic formats as appropriate. Authors retain many rights under the Taylor & Francis rights policies, which can be found at www.informaworld.com/authors_journals_copyright_position. Authors are themselves responsible for obtaining permission to reproduce copyright material from other sources.

Typescripts: These should be double spaced, with adequate margins, and numbered throughout. The title page of an article should contain only (1) the title of the paper, the name(s) and address(es) of the author(s); (2) a short title not exceeding 40 letters and spaces, which will be used for page headlines; (3) name, address, fax, and e-mail address of the author to whom correspondence and proofs should be sent. The article should have an abstract of no more than 150 words and 5 keywords.

List of references: The list of references should be typed with double spacing, and in alphabetical order of author's name. Sample references:

Striano, T., Stahl, D., & Cleveland, A. (2009). Taking a closer look at social and cognitive skills: A weekly longitudinal assessment between 7 and 10 months of age. *European Journal of Developmental Psychology, 6*(5), 567–591. doi: 10.1080/17405620701480642

Winne, P. H., & Alexander, P. A. (Eds.). (2006). *Handbook of educational psychology* (2nd ed.). London: Routledge.

Hopkins, B., & Butterworth, G. (1997). Dynamical systems approaches to the development of action. In G. Bremner, A. Slater, & G. Butterworth (Eds.), *Infant development: Recent advances* (pp. 55–74). Hove, UK: Psychology Press.

The *European Journal of Developmental Psychology* now offers an iOpenAccess option for authors. For more information, see: www.tandf.co.uk/journals/iopenaccess.asp

The *European Journal of Developmental Psychology* is published for the European Society for Developmental Psychology by Psychology Press, an Informa business.

Disclaimer: Psychology Press makes every effort to ensure the accuracy of all the information (the "Content") contained in its publications. However, Psychology Press and its agents and licensors make no representations or warranties whatsoever as to the accuracy, completeness or suitability for any purpose of the Content and disclaim all such representations and warranties whether express or implied to the maximum extent permitted by law. Any views expressed in this publication are the views of the authors and are not the views of Psychology Press.

Back issues: Taylor & Francis retains a three-year back issue stock of journals. Older volumes are held by our official stockists: Periodicals Service Company, 11 Main Street, Germantown, NY 12526, USA to whom all orders and enquiries should be addressed. Tel: +1 518 537 4700; Fax: +1 518 537 5899; E-mail: psc@periodicals.com; URL: http://www.periodicals.com/tandf.html

Abstracted/Indexed in: Current Contents/Social and Behavioral Sciences (CC/S&BS); European Reference Index for the Humanities (ERIH); PsycINFO; PubsHub; Social Sciences Citation Index (SSCI).

Typeset by KnowledgeWorks Global Limited, Chennai, India.

In all locations, national identity was assessed using the Strength of Identification Scale (Barrett, 2007) involving six questions pertaining to the degree of national identification, affect toward national identity, positive and negative internalization of aspects of national identity, the importance of national identification, and national pride. Attitudes toward in-groups and out-groups were examined using the attribution task developed by Barrett and colleagues (e.g., Barrett, Wilson, & Lyons, 2003; Reizábal, Valencia, & Barrett, 2004). In this task, the participants are asked to assign different positive and negative qualities to citizens of different countries including their own country or national group, the "traditional enemy" out-group, and other more neutral out-groups. Attitudes were also assessed using general affect questions about how much the children liked each of the target groups. The data were analysed and are reported using a common pre-set procedure, as well as procedures specific to the individual national locations according to each team's particular theoretical and methodological orientation and the specificities of their own local national context.

The first paper by Barrett and Oppenheimer provides an overview of the empirical and theoretical background against which the studies were designed. This paper also reports the full details of the common measures and procedures that were employed by all of the research teams. This opening paper is then followed by six further papers, which separately report the findings from the data that were collected in England, Bosnia, Northern Ireland, northern Cyprus, southern Cyprus and the Basque Country. The final paper by Oppenheimer then reports the results of the full cross-national comparative analyses.

As the papers in this special issue reveal, the development of national identifications and national attitudes shows considerable cross-national variation as a function of the specific sociohistorical contexts within which children develop. These studies, considered together, indicate the need for developmental theorizing within this area to avoid simplistic conclusions based on data that have only been collected within one specific location, to acknowledge the crucial role of sociohistorical settings in children's development within this domain, and to adopt a much broader cross-national comparative perspective when attempting to address questions concerning how children's national identifications and national attitudes develop within real-world settings.

REFERENCES

Barrett, M. (2007). *Children's knowledge, beliefs and feelings about nations and national groups.* Hove, UK: Psychology Press.

Barrett, M., Wilson, H., & Lyons, E. (2003). The development of national in-group bias: English children's attributions of characteristics to English, American and German people. *British Journal of Developmental Psychology, 21,* 193–220.

Bennett, M., Barrett, M., Karakozov, R., Kipiani, G., Lyons, E., Pavlenko, V., et al. (2004). Young children's evaluations of the ingroup and of outgroups: A multi-national study. *Social Development, 13*, 124–141.

Bennett, M., Lyons, E., Sani, F., & Barrett, M. (1998). Children's subjective identification with the group and ingroup favoritism. *Developmental Psychology, 34*, 902–909.

Bigler, R. S., Brown, C. S., & Markell, M. (2001). When groups are not created equal: Effects of group status on the formation of intergroup attitudes in children. *Child Development, 72*, 1151–1162.

Bigler, R. S., Jones, L. C., & Lobliner, D. B. (1997). Social categorization and the formation of intergroup attitudes in children. *Child Development, 68*, 530–543.

Masangkay, Z. S., Villorente, F. F., Somcio, R. S., Reyes, E. S., & Taylor, D. M. (1972). The development of ethnic group perception. *The Journal of Genetic Psychology, 121*, 263–270.

Nesdale, D., & Flesser, D. (2001). Social identity and the development of children's group attitudes. *Child Development, 72*, 506–517.

Oppenheimer, L. (in press). National identification of Dutch youth: An exploratory study. *Journal of Adolescence.*

Poppe, E., & Linssen, H. (1999) Ingroup favouritism and the reflection of realistic dimensions of differences between national states in Central and Eastern European nationality stereotypes. *British Journal of Social Psychology, 38*, 85–102.

Reizábal, L., Valencia, J., & Barrett, M. (2004). National identifications and attitudes to national ingroups and outgroups among children living in the Basque Country. *Infant and Child Development, 13*, 1–20.

Teichman, Y. (2001). The development of Israeli children's images of Jews and Arabs and their expression in human figure drawings. *Developmental Psychology, 37*, 749–761.

EUROPEAN JOURNAL OF DEVELOPMENTAL PSYCHOLOGY
2011, 8 (1), 5–24

Ψ Psychology Press
Taylor & Francis Group

Findings, theories and methods in the study of children's national identifications and national attitudes

Martyn Barrett[1] and Louis Oppenheimer[2]

[1]Department of Psychology, University of Surrey, Guildford, Surrey, UK
[2]Department of Developmental Psychology, University of Amsterdam, Amsterdam, The Netherlands

This paper reviews some of the relevant background findings against which the empirical studies reported in this special issue were designed. Particular attention is given to previous findings on the development of children's national knowledge, national attitudes and national identifications. The paper also reviews five existing theories, which have been proposed to explain the development of children's intergroup attitudes: cognitive-developmental theory (Aboud, 1988, 2008), social identity development theory (Nesdale, 2004, 2008), social identity theory (Tajfel, 1978; Tajfel & Turner, 1986), societal-social-cognitive-motivational theory (Barrett, 2007, 2009; Barrett & Davis, 2008) and integrative developmental-contextual theory (Bar-Tal & Teichman, 2005; Teichman & Bar-Tal, 2008). The paper concludes by describing the shared methodology that was utilized by all of the following studies that are reported in this special issue. These studies were designed to examine how children's attitudes to other nations develop within a range of different national contexts, some of which have not experienced violent conflict in the recent past (England, The Netherlands) but others of which have recently experienced, or still are experiencing, conflict, violence or warfare (Basque Country, Bosnia, north and south Cyprus, Northern Ireland, Israel).

Keywords: National identity; National attitudes; Intergroup attitudes; Developmental theories; Methodology.

This special issue of the *European Journal of Developmental Psychology* is devoted to a series of studies that have emerged from a multi-national

Correspondence should be addressed to Martyn Barrett, Department of Psychology, University of Surrey, Guildford, Surrey GU2 7XH, UK. E-mail: m.barrett@surrey.ac.uk

http://www.psypress.com/edp   DOI: 10.1080/17405629.2010.533955

research project that investigated children's national identifications and attitudes to national in-groups and out-groups as determinants of the understanding of enemy and the presence of enemy images (Barrett, 2007; Oppenheimer, 2005, 2006). One of the distinctive features of this project is that data were collected in a range of different national contexts, some of which have not experienced violent conflict in the recent past (England and The Netherlands) but others of which have recently experienced, or still are experiencing, conflict, violence or warfare (Basque Country, Bosnia, north and south Cyprus, Northern Ireland and Israel). In total, children from 12 national groups participated, including Jewish and Arab children (Israel), Bosnian and Serbian children (Bosnia), Catholic and Protestant children (Northern Ireland), Greek-Cypriot and Turkish-Cypriot children (Cyprus), Basque and Spanish children (the Basque Country), and Dutch and English children (The Netherlands and England).[1] The project was based on the assumption that children's national identifications and attitudes are related to the everyday patterns of discourse and practices that occur within the particular sociohistorical settings in which they are living, and for this reason the contrast in the development of children growing up within relatively peaceful versus conflict-ridden contexts was expected to be particularly marked.

In this paper, we describe some of the relevant background findings and theories in the field, so that readers are able to situate the present work within its broader research context. This paper also describes the shared methodology that was employed by all of the studies reported in this special issue.

PREVIOUS FINDINGS ON CHILDREN'S NATIONAL KNOWLEDGE, NATIONAL ATTITUDES AND NATIONAL IDENTIFICATIONS

Studies exploring children's geographical knowledge of their own country have typically found that such knowledge begins to be acquired from about 5 years of age (Barrett, 2005a, 2007; Jahoda, 1963a; Piaget & Weil, 1951), with the mass media (especially television) and travel being important sources of information (Gould & White, 1986). Children's geographical knowledge of other countries starts to develop at a slightly later age, with a significant increase in such knowledge occurring at about 8 years

---

[1] In this special issue, the data collected in The Netherlands and in Israel are not reported separately in individual papers. However, these data are included in the cross-national comparative analyses reported in the final paper by Oppenheimer.

(Barrett, 1996; Jahoda, 1962; Wiegand, 1991a). Children's geographical knowledge of other countries is largely derived from foreign travel, formal teaching at school and television and films, and varies as a function of their social class, nationality, ethnicity and geographical location (Axia, Bremner, Deluca, & Andreasen, 1998; Bourchier, Barrett, & Lyons, 2002; Holloway & Valentine, 2000; Wiegand, 1991a, 1991b).

Most children already know some of the symbolic emblems (e.g., flags, national anthems, etc.) that are used to represent their own country by 5–6 years of age, and this emblematic knowledge continues to develop over subsequent years (Barrett, 2007; Helwig & Prencipe, 1999; Jahoda, 1963b; Moore, Lare, & Wagner, 1985; Weinstein, 1957). There is significant cross-national variability in such knowledge (Barrett et al., 1997), and there are also variations within countries in children's use of, and affect for, national emblems as a function of their language group, ethnicity and gender (Moodie, 1980; Moore et al., 1985).

Other studies that have investigated the development of children's national stereotypes have shown that stereotypes of some groups are acquired already by the age of 5 or 6 (Barrett & Short, 1992; Barrett, Wilson, & Lyons, 2003; Bar-Tal, 1996; Lambert & Klineberg, 1967; Oppenheimer & Hakvoort, 2003), with these stereotypes gradually being elaborated over the next few years so that, by 10 or 11 years, children hold extensive beliefs about the typical physical features, clothing, habits, psychological and personality traits of a large number of different national groups. Children obtain their beliefs about other national groups from many different sources, including television, films, books, school work, teachers, parents, visits to other countries, and personal contact with foreigners (Barrett, 2007; Barrett & Short, 1992; Bar-Tal, 1997; Holloway & Valentine, 2000; Lambert & Klineberg, 1967).

Schools, in particular, usually provide a great deal of explicit teaching to children about their own nation via the curriculum in subjects such as history, geography, civic/citizenship education, language and literature. It is therefore especially noteworthy that school curricula and textbooks in these subjects frequently contain ethnocentric biases, with the child's own nation usually being presented in a highly positive light compared with other nations (Apple, 1993; Schleicher & Kozma, 1992).

Children's attitudes to and feelings about other nations are often idiosyncratic before about 7 years of age. However, an exception occurs in the case of those nations which are the "traditional enemies" of the child's own country, which are often disliked from an earlier age (Barrett, 2007; Jahoda, 1962; Oppenheimer & Hakvoort, 2003; Piaget & Weil, 1951; Teichman, 2001). Indeed, in countries that have experienced warfare, extreme negativity may be displayed towards enemy groups as early as 2 or 3 years of age (Bar-Tal, 1996; Bar-Tal & Teichman, 2005; Povrzanović, 1997). From 7 years onwards, many children exhibit a preference for their own country and national group over all others, and express strong national pride, with in-group preference and national pride sometimes strengthening still further through middle childhood (Barrett & Short, 1992; Hess & Torney, 1967; Jaspers, van de Geer, Tajfel, & Johnson, 1972; Johnson, Middelton, & Tajfel, 1970). However, some other countries and national groups may still be very positively liked and, in a few cases, may even be preferred over the child's own country or national group (Middleton, Tajfel, & Johnson, 1970; Moore et al., 1985; Tajfel, Jahoda, Nemeth, Rim, & Johnson, 1972). Hence, contrary to popular notions, in-group favouritism and out-group denigration are *not* universal phenomena in this domain.

In addition, children's attitudes towards national groups display considerable variation in how they develop through middle childhood. For example, with increasing age, children's national attitudes sometimes become more positive, sometimes more negative, sometimes more negative before becoming more positive again, sometimes more positive before becoming more negative again, and sometimes children's national attitudes do not show any changes at all across middle childhood (Barrett, 2007; Lambert & Klineberg, 1967). Furthermore, different developmental profiles may be exhibited depending on the particular national out-group involved. These differential patterns seem to be related to a number of factors, including the perceived characteristics of the target group involved, the national context within which the child is growing up, and the child's own specific geographical, ethnic and linguistic position within that national context (Barrett, 2007).

As far as children's national identifications are concerned, by the age of 6, most children do usually acknowledge their membership of their own national group, but their strength of subjective identification with that group varies at this early age (Barrett, 2007). There is also a great deal of variation in the subsequent development of children's national identifications. This variation seems to depend on the specific country in which the child lives, the child's geographical location within that country, the child's ethnicity, the use of language in the family home, and the child's language of schooling (Barrett, 2005b, 2007). The strength of national identification is usually correlated with the child's general affect towards the national in-group (Barrett, 2007; Barrett, Lyons & del Valle, 2004). However, the strength of national identification is only sometimes related to the positive distinctiveness that is attributed to the in-group over out-groups as measured using trait attribution tasks (Barrett, 2007).

THEORETICAL ACCOUNTS OF THE DEVELOPMENT OF INTERGROUP ATTITUDES IN CHILDHOOD

Several theoretical accounts have been proposed to explain the development of children's intergroup attitudes. Here, we focus on the five theories that are the most pertinent to the studies on children's national attitudes reported in this special issue.

Cognitive-developmental theory

Cognitive-developmental theory (CDT) has been primarily expounded and elaborated by Aboud (1988, 2008; Aboud & Amato, 2001; Doyle & Aboud, 1995; Doyle, Beaudet, & Aboud, 1988). She argues that children's intergroup attitudes are driven by their underlying cognitive and sociocognitive development. Strongly Piagetian in orientation, CDT postulates that there is a watershed in the development of children's intergroup attitudes at the age of about 6–7 years. Prior to this age, Aboud suggests, children's egocentricity and affective processes dominate their responses to people from other national, ethnic and racial groups, with the result that they exhibit pronounced in-group bias and negative prejudice against out-groups. These biases are hypothesized to peak at 6–7 years, after which they decline. Aboud argues that, at 6–7 years, children attribute mainly positive traits to their own in-group and mainly negative traits to out-groups; however, between 6–7 and 11–12 years, children increasingly attribute more negative traits to the in-group and more positive traits to out-groups. This results in a reduction in levels of both in-group bias and out-group prejudice. These shifts are hypothesized to be driven by the development of the child's underlying cognitive and sociocognitive skills.

In her more recent formulations, Aboud (2008; Aboud & Amato, 2001) has acknowledged that socialization factors may sometimes influence children's intergroup attitudes, particularly those of ethnic-minority children who do not always exhibit out-group prejudice before 6–7 years. However, she argues that the effectiveness of parental discourse, media representations and educational input in altering children's attitudes depends on the child's cognitive mindset, with children's own cognitive abilities determining which social inputs are influential.

Because of its postulation of a single normative pattern of development grounded in a universal sequence of cognitive-developmental changes, CDT has difficulty in explaining the sheer variety of different developmental patterns that children's attitudes to national groups display during middle childhood (Barrett, 2007; Lambert & Klineberg, 1967). Aboud and Amato (2001, p. 78) themselves also acknowledge that CDT lacks a clear explanation of why children differentiate between out-groups, attaching positive evaluations to some out-groups and negative evaluations to others.

Social identity development theory

In recent years, social identity development theory (SIDT) has been put forward by Nesdale (2004, 2008) as an alternative to CDT, and the theory does indeed make very different predictions from CDT. SIDT postulates that there are four phases in the development of children's intergroup attitudes. Before 2–3 years of age, cues about people's racial, ethnic and national group memberships are not yet salient to the child. The second phase starts at about 3 years, when awareness of these cues begins to emerge. In addition, during this second phase, the child acquires the awareness that he or she is a member of the in-group. SIDT postulates that, during the third phase, which commences at about 4 years, the child focuses on, and prefers, the in-group over out-groups. During this phase, the child does not dislike or reject out-groups. Instead, the in-group is merely preferred over other groups. The fourth phase of development postulated by SIDT begins at about 7 years, when the child's focus shifts away from the in-group and towards out-groups and negative prejudice against out-groups begins to emerge. However, Nesdale argues that not all children enter this final phase. Whether they do so depends on whether the child internalizes prejudices current among members of the in-group. The likelihood of this occurring is driven by the strength of the child's subjective identification with the in-group, how widespread the negative attitudes are among members of the in-group, and the extent to which in-group members feel under threat from the out-group concerned. SIDT therefore predicts that negative prejudice against "enemy" nations will arise after the age of 7 in those countries that perceive themselves to be under threat from other nations and where negative attitudes to the "enemy" nations are widely held by in-group members.

CDT and SIDT are polarized in the predictions that they make about the development of prejudice, with CDT proposing that out-group prejudice increases up to 6–7 years and then decreases, and with SIDT proposing that it is only after 7 years that prejudice starts to develop (and even then may not develop in all children). CDT has drawn much of its evidence from studies that have used trait attribution tasks to test children's explicit attitudes towards groups (e.g., Doyle & Aboud, 1995; Doyle et al., 1988). One of the potential problems with such tasks is that children can tailor their responses, particularly where there are social norms against the expression of prejudice. Nesdale argues that the apparent reduction in prejudice across middle childhood is a result of children's increasing awareness of the unacceptability of openly expressing prejudice against out-groups, rather than of prejudice reduction *per se*. He suggests that alternative measures of children's implicit rather than explicit attitudes are therefore required to test between the two theories. However, evidence from recent studies using implicit measures (e.g., Davis, Leman, & Barrett, 2007; Dunham, Baron, & Banaji, 2006) do not support SIDT, with levels of implicit prejudice either remaining steady after 6–7 years of age or declining rather than increasing after this age. SIDT also has difficulty explaining why, in countries that have experienced inter-ethnic conflict or warfare, extreme negativity can be exhibited towards enemy groups at the age of 2–3 years (Bar-Tal, 1996; Bar-Tal & Teichman, 2005; Povrzanović, 1997).

Social identity theory

Social identity theory (SIT) does not make predictions about age-linked developmental changes in children's attitudes, but it does make predictions about the circumstances under which in-group bias and out-group prejudice will occur. SIT was developed by Tajfel (1978; Tajfel & Turner, 1986), who argued that when individuals internalize a social group membership as part of their self-concept, those individuals are motivated to view that social group in a positive way. In order to do this, the in-group is compared against out-groups using dimensions of comparison that yield more positive representations of the in-group than of out-groups. The positive distinctiveness which is ascribed to the in-group over the out-groups on these chosen dimensions is then used as a source of positive self-esteem. However, SIT postulates that this only occurs under certain conditions. First, the individual must have internalized the social group membership as part of his or her self-concept. If internalization has not occurred, or if identification with the group is weak, then these effects will not occur. Second, the comparison out-groups must be relevant to the in-group's own self-definition. If out-groups are not relevant to how the in-group views itself, then in-group favouritism and/or out-group denigration will not occur. Third, the situation in which these social comparisons take place must allow comparisons to be made on dimensions that are relevant for the in-group's own self-definition.

In addition, Tajfel and Turner (1986) argued that, where an out-group is perceived to have a clearly superior status to the in-group, alternative strategies need to be used instead to achieve positive self-esteem. These include leaving the in-group (individual mobility), redefining the in-group or changing the dimensions that are being used for the comparison (social creativity), or changing the social structure itself (social competition). Individual mobility may occur when group boundaries are viewed as being permeable, while social creativity and social competition may occur when group boundaries are viewed as being impermeable. Social competition is most likely to occur when status differentials are perceived to be illegitimate or the status of the out-group is perceived to be unstable. Because the strategy depends on perceptions of group boundary permeability and the legitimacy and stability of status differentials, SIT proposes that intergroup attitudes and behaviours vary depending on a wide range of different factors.

More recent research inspired by SIT (e.g., Crocker & Quinn, 2001; Ellemers & Barreto, 2001; Ellemers, Spears, & Doosje, 1999; Mummendey, Kessler, Klink, & Mielke, 1999; Simon, 2004) has examined the consequences of belonging to a social group that is perceived to be under threat. This work has revealed that members of threatened groups tend to have higher levels of identification with the in-group, tend to show higher levels of out-group prejudice and/or in-group favouritism, tend to be more sensitive to status differentials between groups, and tend to perceive the in-group as being more homogeneous and more cohesive. However, these effects only occur among individuals with high levels of in-group identification; individuals with weak identifications may simply disidentify with the group still further under conditions of threat. This body of research therefore predicts that patterns of national identifications and attitudes will differ in relatively peaceful countries where the national group is not perceived to be under threat versus countries characterized by intergroup conflict, violence or warfare.

SIT can explain why children belonging to different groups display different intergroup attitudes depending on their strength of identification with the in-group, the perceived status of the in-group and perceptions of threat. It also helps to explain why attitudes towards out-groups which vary in status are differentiated so that attitudes towards one out-group may be different from attitudes towards another out-group.

Societal-social-cognitive-motivational theory

Societal-social-cognitive-motivational theory (SSCMT) has recently been put forward by Barrett (2007, 2009; Barrett & Davis, 2008). Like SIT, this theory does not make predictions about the particular ages at which in-group favouritism or out-group prejudice occur. Instead, this theory attempts to integrate within a single overarching framework all of the influences that impact on children's intergroup attitudes.

SSCMT is represented diagrammatically in Figure 1. SSCMT starts from the observation that the child always develops within a particular societal niche characterized by specific historical, geographical, economic and political circumstances. These circumstances define the relationships between the child's in-groups and salient out-groups, their status differentials and their history of peaceful coexistence and/or conflict. Adult

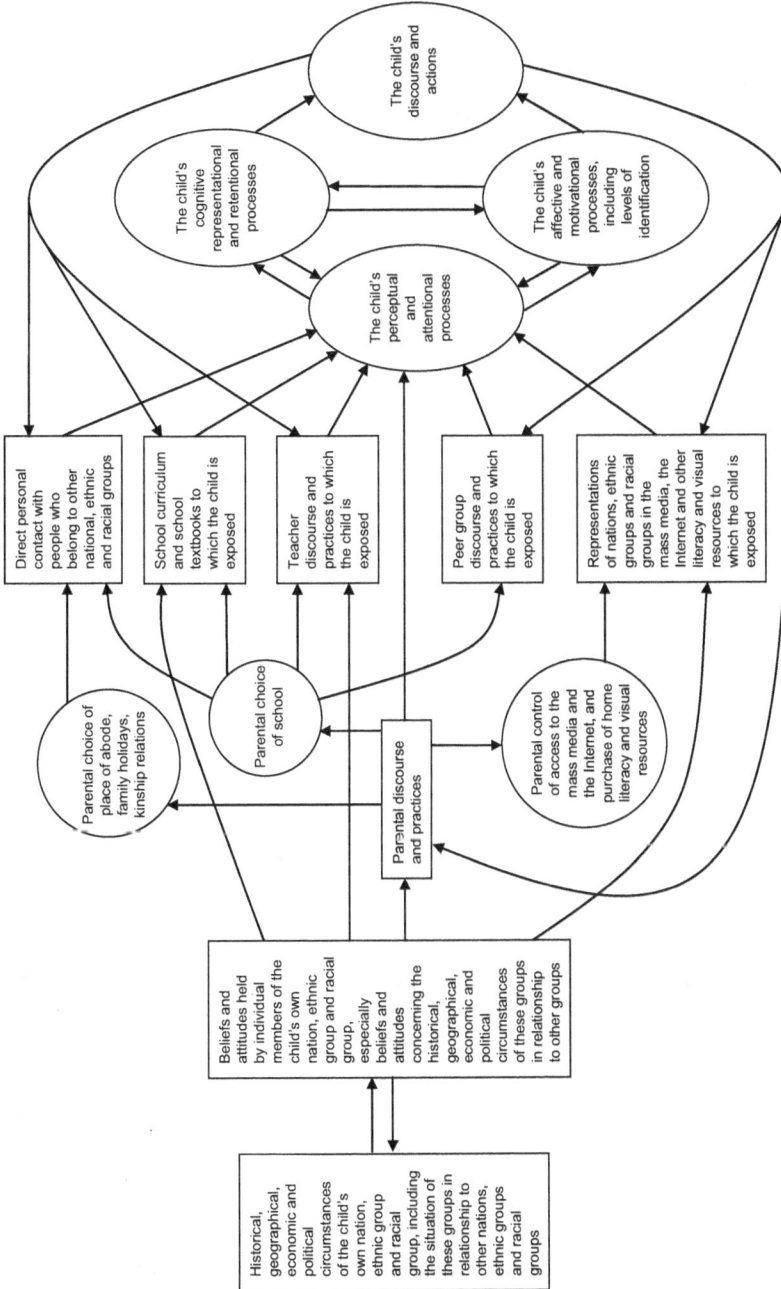

Figure 1. Societal-social-cognitive-motivational theory (SSCMT; adapted from Barrett, 2007).

members of the child's society hold their own beliefs and attitudes concerning these circumstances, and these can drive their behaviours. From the point of view of the developing child, the most relevant individuals here are parents, teachers and the people who produce materials for school curricula, textbooks and the mass media.

SSCMT proposes that parents' discourse and actions can directly influence their children's developing intergroup attitudes. However, parents can also have indirect effects, because they determine where the family lives, where they go on holiday and the kinship relations of the child (all of which may affect the nature of the child's personal contact with people from other national, ethnic and racial groups). Parents also determine which school the child attends, and hence the educational curriculum, textbooks, teachers and peer group to which the child is exposed. The school itself can also influence the child's personal contact with people from other national, ethnic and racial groups (depending on its own ethnic and racial mix). In addition, parents buy goods for the family home such as books, televisions, computers connected to the internet, etc. In the case of younger children, parents may also control access to some of these information sources.

Hence, there are many sources of information about other groups available to the child: personal contact with members of those groups; the school curriculum and textbooks; teacher discourse and practices; parental discourse and practices; peer group discourse and practices; and representations of other groups in the mass media (Barrett, 2007; Bar-Tal & Teichman, 2005; Oppenheimer, 2010). However, which information sources are actually attended to by the child are influenced by the child's own perceptual and attentional processes. These in turn are influenced by the child's cognitive, affective and motivational processes (including levels of identification with national, ethnic and racial in-groups). Hence, different sets of environmental factors may be influential for different children depending on their own psychological characteristics. In addition, the child's own discourse and actions may be responded to by parents, teachers, peers, etc., and these actors may either provide further information to the child, challenge what the child has said or done, or punish or praise the child.

SSCMT postulates that different constellations of factors are the primary drivers of intergroup attitudes in different children, depending on their own psychological characteristics, the groups to which they belong, and the particular societal contexts in which they live. In other words, SSCMT proposes that the relative weightings that may be attached to the arrows in Figure 1 vary from one child to another, and from one sociohistorical setting to another. Both cognitive development and social identity processes may play important roles, as CDT and SIT suggest, but SSCMT proposes that these factors can be overridden in some contexts by other factors such as parental discourse, media representations or educational influences. Hence, SSCMT postulates that there is substantial variability in the development of children's intergroup attitudes depending on the specific contexts in which they live.

Integrative developmental-contextual theory

Integrative developmental-contextual theory (IDCT) has been developed by Bar-Tal and Teichman (2005; Teichman & Bar-Tal, 2008) to account for the development of children's intergroup attitudes within societal contexts characterized by intractable intergroup conflict. The theory is therefore especially relevant to several of the empirical studies reported in this special issue.

IDCT proposes that when there is serious and ongoing conflict between the in-group and an out-group, in-group members acquire a shared psychological intergroup repertoire (SPIR) in relationship to that out-group. This repertoire consists of stereotypes of the out-group, prejudice, associated emotions and behavioural intentions towards the out-group. The acquisition of a SPIR is influenced by affective states, cognitive development and identity development. While all three factors can potentially operate at all ages, the prevailing social context affects their relative salience. In contexts involving intractable conflict, affective states tend to be the dominant factor in the preschool years and, so, between the ages of 2 and 6, negative affect dominates, resulting in strong negative feelings towards members of the enemy out-group. Once established, this kind of SPIR can then swamp out possible cognitive effects in later childhood. The result is that prejudice against the enemy nation is acquired early (at 2–3 years of age), no reduction in prejudice takes place during middle childhood (7–9 years), and during early adolescence (10 years plus) identity concerns and their motivational correlates may lead to a further increase in hostility towards the enemy out-group. The content of the SPIR itself is transmitted by socialization agents, including parents, the mass media and the school.

According to IDCT, once it has been formed, a SPIR will influence the relative salience of affective, cognitive and identity factors, so that the SPIR and these factors reinforce each other, consolidating negative attitudes and prejudice towards the enemy. Extreme ethnocentrism results, which is highly resistant to change. For this reason, attempts at intervention and the amelioration of negative attitudes (e.g., through education) may be ineffective.

Thus, according to IDCT, in societies characterized by intractable conflict, attitudes towards the enemy out-group develop in a different way from the way in which attitudes to other neutral out-groups develop, and from the way in which intergroup attitudes develop in peaceful societies.

Hence, like SIT and SSCMT, IDCT emphasizes that the development of intergroup attitudes does not follow a universal trajectory.

Bar-Tal and Teichman (2005; see also Teichman & Bar-Tal, 2008) provided a wealth of evidence that, in Israel, which is a context characterized by an intractable conflict between Jews and Arabs, Jewish children do indeed exhibit high levels of prejudice towards Arabs at an early age, do not moderate their prejudice across the years of middle childhood, and show a further elevation in this prejudice in early adolescence. These studies also reveal that majority Jewish and minority Arab children in Israel display different patterns of attitude development. Bar-Tal and Teichman argue that the Jewish children's attitudes are driven mainly by Israel's ongoing conflict with its neighbouring states, whereas the Arab children's attitudes are driven primarily by their minority status within Israel.

IDCT and SSCMT clearly have considerable conceptual overlap but different foci, with the former theory providing a specific account of children's development within contexts characterized by intractable inter-group conflict, and the latter theory providing a more general account of the full range of possible factors that may impact on children's development across all types of societal context. Despite this difference in focus, the two theories share several common postulates. For example, both theories emphasize: (i) the absence of universal developmental trajectories and the existence of pervasive variability in the development of intergroup attitudes; (ii) the role of parents, the mass media and education in transmitting representations of prevailing intergroup relations to the child; (iii) the possible influence of cognitive, affective, motivational and identity factors in the development of intergroup attitudes; (iv) the idea that cognitive, affective, motivational and identity factors can affect the uptake of information from the environment; and (v) the idea that different factors and causal pathways may dominate in a child's development depending on the specific societal setting within which that child is living.

THE SHARED METHODOLOGY USED BY THE STUDIES REPORTED IN THIS SPECIAL ISSUE

The present multi-national study was conducted against this empirical and theoretical backdrop. One of the aims of the study was to examine the extent to which the development of children's attitudes to other nations varies across different societal contexts. This comparative aim required identical methodology to be used with all groups of children to permit formal comparisons to be made. The shared methodology which was used included the following measures.

Strength of Identification Scale

The Strength of Identification Scale (SoIS; Barrett, 2007) is a scale which has been developed to measure the strength of national, ethnic, racial or religious identification in children and adolescents. It consists of a short set of questions administered in an interview format to 5- to 11-year-olds (with response options being written on cards and read out to the child) or in a questionnaire format to 11- to 16-year-olds (with rating scales being used instead to capture responses). The full set of six items in the 5- to 11-year-old version of the scale are as follows (where X represents the targeted identity):

1. *Degree of identification*
   Question: *Which one of these do you think best describes you?*
   Response options: *very X, quite X, a little bit X, not at all X*
2. *Pride*
   Question: How proud are you of being X?
   Response options: very proud, quite proud, a little bit proud, not at all proud
3. *Importance*
   Question: How important is it to you that you are X?
   Response options: very important, quite important, not very important, not important at all
4. *Feeling*
   Question: How do you feel about being X?
   Response options: very happy, quite happy, neutral, quite sad, very sad (administered using a set of five "smiley" faces)
5. *Negative internalization*
   Question: How you would feel if someone said something bad about X people?
   Response options: very happy, quite happy, neutral, quite sad, very sad (administered using a set of five "smiley" faces)
6. *Positive internalization*
   Question: How you would feel if someone said something good about X people?
   Response options: very happy, quite happy, neutral, quite sad, very sad (administered using a set of five "smiley" faces)

The questions are scored so that low scores represent low levels of identification, and high scores represent high levels of identification. Because the questions use a mixture of 4- and 5-point scales, either the item scores are standardized before they are averaged, or the scores on the

4-point scales are rescaled onto 5-point scales before averaging.[2] All six items need not be used, particularly where the wording of a particular question is awkward and/or unnatural for the identity that is being tested.

The SoIS has previously been used to measure the strength of national, ethnic, racial and religious identification in various populations, including national identifications in white English 11- to 16-year-olds (Dixon, 2002; Forrest & Barrett, 2001), national identifications in 6- to 11-year-olds in Scotland and Wales (Penny, Barrett, & Lyons, 2001; Trimby, 2005), national and ethnic identifications in an ethnically mixed group of 11- to 16-year-olds in London (Alexander, 2002), religious identifications in Muslim, Hindu and Christian 5- to 11-year-olds in England (Takriti, 2002), national, ethnic and religious identifications in English, Indian and Pakistani 7- to 11-year-olds (Vethanayagam & Barrett, 2007), racial and national identifications in 5- to 9-year-old children in England (Davis et al., 2007), national identifications in Iranian 11- to 17-year-olds in England and Iran (Sahlabadi, 2002), national identifications in 12- to 18-year-olds in Germany (Maehr, 2005), and ethnic and religious identifications in Albanian 8- to 13-year-olds in Greece (Manouka, 2001). These studies have found that SoIS item scores always load onto a single factor (eigenvalues ranging between 2.02 and 3.30; percentage of variance explained ranging between 40.8 and 80.1) and scale reliably (Cronbach's alpha ranging between .60 and .91, with the sole exception of young white children's racial identifications in the study by Davis et al., 2007, where the reliability was only .41). In addition, the test–retest reliability of the SoIS over an eight-week period has been found to be .68 (Barrett, 2007).

In the studies that are reported in this special issue, the 5- to 11-year-old version of the SoIS was used to assess the strength of children's national identifications. In order to control possible order effects, for each child individually, the order of administration of the six questions was randomized. In addition, to avoid possible left–right response biases, response cards were laid out in sequence always keeping the "don't know" card on the far right but reversing the order of layout of the other cards within each set across successive children.

The trait attribution task and the affect questions

Attitudes to in-groups and out-groups were measured using a trait attribution task (taken from Barrett et al., 1997). The task used a set of 12 cards, on each of which one of the following traits was written: *clean, dirty, friendly, unfriendly, smart, stupid, hard working, lazy, happy, sad,*

---

[2]In rescaling, $1 = 1$, $2 = 2.33$, $3 = 3.66$, and $4 = 5$.

honest and *dishonest*. The cards were randomly ordered for each individual child. The pile of cards was shown to the child so that he or she could see the word on the first card, and the following instructions were given:

> *Here are some cards with words on them that describe people. So, we can say that some people are [word on first card].* (First card removed, and child shown the second card.) *And some people are [word on second card].* (Second card removed.) *And some people are [word on third card]. Right? Now, what I want you to do is to go through all these words one by one, and I want you to sort out those words which you think can be used to describe X people* (where X represented the name of the target national group). *Can you do that for me please?* (Child given the complete set of cards.) *Sort out the words which you think describe X people.*

When the child had finished the task, the cards were gathered up in a randomly ordered pile, ready for testing the next target nationality. The child was then asked two further questions to assess general affect towards the target group of people:

> *Now, I just want to ask you one more thing about X people. Do you like or dislike X people?* (If the child said that he or she liked or disliked them, the second question was then given.) *How much? Do you like/dislike them a lot or a little?*

At the end of this sequence of questions, the child was told:

> *Right now, let's do the same thing again, but this time thinking about X people* (where X was the name of the next target group to be tested). *Can you sort out for me those words which you think can be used to describe X people?*

In total, the children in the present sequence of studies were given the above task and questions in relationship to their own national in-group, an out-group that was a "traditional enemy" of their own in-group, plus two relatively neutral out-groups. The order in which the four target national groups were tested was randomized for each individual child.

The wordings used in the trait attribution task and the affect questions have been found to work well with children in a range of different national settings (Bennett et al., 2004; Bennett, Lyons, Sani, & Barrett, 1998; Castelli, Cadinu, & Barrett, 2002; Giménez, Canto, Fernández, & Barrett, 2003; Reizábal, Valencia, & Barrett, 2004; Vila, del Valle, Perera, Monreal, & Barrett, 1998). The quantitative scores that were derived from the trait attribution task included the total number of positive traits and the total number of negative traits attributed to each individual target group. In addition, by subtracting the number of negative traits from the number of positive traits, an overall positivity score was derived for each target group. The responses to the affect questions were scored on a 5-point Likert scale ranging from *like a lot* (5) to *dislike a lot* (1) with neutral responses being scored at the midpoint (3).

Procedure

The above tasks were administered to the children as follows. Each child was interviewed individually in a quiet room in their school. After establishing rapport, it was explained that the interviewer was interested in what they thought about certain things and that the child would be asked to complete some tasks and answer some questions. Each child was reassured that they were not being tested, that there were no good or bad answers, and that no one other than the interviewer would know what they had said. The children were then asked to give their age, gender, and ethnicity. Their responses to these initial questions, as well as their responses on all the tasks, were recorded on individual response sheets.

Because the research took place in different languages, backtranslation procedures were used. The initial draft of the tasks was drawn up in the English language, and this draft was translated into the target language by one translator, and then backtranslated into English by a different translator. The product was compared with the original English version to ascertain whether any changes in meaning had occurred. If they had, the translators discussed the change in meaning and agreed on an appropriate translation in the target language.

CONCLUSION

In this paper, we have provided a brief overview of some of the previous research findings in this field and of the five principal theories that may be applied to explain developmental phenomena in this domain. These overviews should enable the reader to locate the following papers in this special issue within their broader research context. In this paper, we have also described the measures and procedures which were used in the studies reported in the following papers. These papers report and interpret the findings obtained in the following countries: England, Bosnia, Northern Ireland, northern Cyprus, southern Cyprus, and the Basque Country. The sequence of papers ends with a final paper reporting the findings of the cross-national comparative analyses, which also incorporate the data collected in The Netherlands and Israel.

REFERENCES

Aboud, F. E. (1988). *Children and prejudice*. Oxford, UK: Blackwell.

Aboud, F. E. (2008). A social-cognitive developmental theory of prejudice. In S. M. Quintana & C. McKown (Eds.), *The handbook of race, racism and the developing child* (pp. 55–71). Hoboken, NJ: Wiley.

Aboud, F. E., & Amato, M. (2001). Developmental and socialization influences on intergroup bias. In R. Brown & S. L. Gaertner (Eds.), *Blackwell handbook of social psychology: Intergroup processes* (pp. 65–85). Oxford, UK: Blackwell.

Alexander, E. (2002). *National and ethnic identity in British adolescents*. Unpublished BSc dissertation, University of Surrey, UK.

Apple, M. (1993). *Official knowledge: Democratic education in a conservative age*. London, UK: Routledge.

Axia, G., Bremner, J. G., Deluca, P., & Andreasen, G. (1998). Children drawing Europe: The effects of nationality, age and teaching. *British Journal of Developmental Psychology, 16*, 423–437.

Barrett, M. (1996). English children's acquisition of a European identity. In G. Breakwell & E. Lyons (Eds.), *Changing European identities: Social psychological analyses of social change* (pp. 349–369). Oxford, UK: Butterworth-Heinemann.

Barrett, M. (2005a). Children's understanding of, and feelings about, countries and national groups. In M. Barrett & E. Buchanan-Barrow (Eds.), *Children's understanding of society* (pp. 251–285). Hove, UK: Psychology Press.

Barrett, M. (2005b). National identities in children and young people. In S. Ding & K. Littleton (Eds.), *Children's personal and social development* (pp. 181–220). Milton Keynes, UK: The Open University/Blackwell Publishing.

Barrett, M. (2007). *Children's knowledge, beliefs and feelings about nations and national groups*. Hove, UK: Psychology Press.

Barrett, M. (2009). The development of children's intergroup attitudes. In A. Hu & M. Byram (Eds.), *Interkulturelle Kompetenz und Fremdsprachliches Lernen: Modelle, Empirie, Evaluation [Intercultural Competence and Foreign Language Learning: Models, Empiricism, Assessment]* (pp. 69–86). Tübingen, Germany: Gunter Narr Verlag.

Barrett, M., & Davis, S. C. (2008). Applying social identity and self-categorization theories to children's racial, ethnic, national and state identifications and attitudes. In S. M. Quintana & C. McKown (Eds.), *The handbook of race, racism and the developing child* (pp. 72–110). Hoboken, NJ: Wiley.

Barrett, M., Lyons, E., Bennett, M., Vila, I., Giménez, A., Arcuri, L., et al. (1997). *Children's beliefs and feelings about their own and other national groups in Europe*. Final Report to the Commission of the European Communities, Directorate-General XII for Science, Research and Development, Human Capital and Mobility (HCM) Programme, Research Network No. CHRX-CT94-0687.

Barrett, M., Lyons, E., & del Valle, A. (2004). The development of national identity and social identity processes: Do social identity theory and self-categorization theory provide useful heuristic frameworks for developmental research? In M. Bennett & F. Sani (Eds.), *The development of the social self* (pp. 159–188). Hove, UK: Psychology Press.

Barrett, M., & Short, J. (1992). Images of European people in a group of 5–10 year old English school children. *British Journal of Developmental Psychology, 10*, 339–363.

Barrett, M., Wilson, H., & Lyons, E. (2003). The development of national in-group bias: English children's attributions of characteristics to English, American and German people. *British Journal of Developmental Psychology, 21*, 193–220.

Bar-Tal, D. (1996). Development of social categories and stereotypes in early childhood: The case of "the Arab" concept formation, stereotype and attitudes by Jewish children in Israel. *International Journal of Intercultural Relations, 20*, 341–370.

Bar-Tal, D. (1997). Formation and change of ethnic and national stereotypes: An integrative model. *International Journal of Intercultural Relations, 21*, 491–523.

Bar-Tal, D., & Teichman, Y. (2005). *Stereotypes and prejudice in conflict: Representations of Arabs in Israeli Jewish society*. Cambridge, UK: Cambridge University Press.

Bennett, M., Barrett, M., Karakozov, R., Kipiani, G., Lyons, E., Pavlenko, V., et al. (2004). Young children's evaluations of the ingroup and of outgroups: A multi-national study. *Social Development, 13*, 124–141.

Bennett, M., Lyons, E., Sani, F., & Barrett, M. (1998). Children's subjective identification with the group and ingroup favoritism. *Developmental Psychology, 34*, 902–909.

Bourchier, A., Barrett, M., & Lyons, E. (2002). The predictors of children's geographical knowledge of other countries. *Journal of Environmental Psychology, 22*, 79–94.

Castelli, L., Cadinu, M., & Barrett, M. (2002). Lo sviluppo degli atteggiamenti nazionali in soggetti in età scolare [The development of national attitudes in subjects of school age]. *Rassegna di Psicologia, 19*, 49–65.

Crocker, J., & Quinn, D. M. (2001). Psychological consequences of devalued identities. In R. Brown & S. L. Gaertner (Eds.), *Blackwell handbook of social psychology: Intergroup processes* (pp. 238–257). Oxford, UK: Blackwell.

Davis, S. C., Leman, P.J., & Barrett, M. (2007). Children's implicit and explicit ethnic group attitudes, ethnic group identification, and self-esteem. *International Journal of Behavioral Development, 31*, 514–525.

Dixon, A. (2002). *Social identity theory and the development of national identity in British adolescents*. Unpublished BSc dissertation, University of Surrey, UK.

Doyle, A. B., & Aboud, F. E. (1995). A longitudinal study of White children's racial prejudice as a social-cognitive development. *Merrill-Palmer Quarterly, 41*, 209–228.

Doyle, A. B., Beaudet, J., & Aboud, F. E. (1988). Developmental patterns in the flexibility of children's ethnic attitudes. *Journal of Cross-Cultural Psychology, 19*, 3–18.

Dunham, Y., Baron, A. S., & Banaji, M. R. (2006). From American city to Japanese village: A cross-cultural investigation of implicit race attitudes. *Child Development, 77*, 1268–1281.

Ellemers, N., & Barreto, M. (2001). The impact of relative group status: Affective, perceptual and behavioral consequences. In R. Brown & S. L. Gaertner (Eds.), *Blackwell handbook of social psychology: Intergroup processes* (pp. 324–343). Oxford, UK: Blackwell.

Ellemers, N., Spears, R., & Doosje, B. (Eds.). (1999). *Social identity*. Oxford, UK: Blackwell.

Forrest, L., & Barrett, M. (2001). *English adolescents' sense of national identity, identity motivations and national historical icons*. Unpublished paper, Department of Psychology, University of Surrey, UK.

Giménez, A., Canto, J. M., Fernández, P., & Barrett, M. (2003). Stereotype development in Andalusian children. *The Spanish Journal of Psychology, 6*, 28–34.

Gould, P., & White, R. (1986). *Mental maps* (2nd ed.). Boston, MA: Allen & Unwin.

Helwig, C. C., & Prencipe, A. (1999). Children's judgments of flags and flag-burning. *Child Development, 70*, 132–143.

Hess, R. D., & Torney, J. V. (1967). *The development of political attitudes in children*. Chicago, IL: Aldine.

Holloway, S. L., & Valentine, G. (2000). Corked hats and Coronation Street: British and New Zealand children's imaginative geographies of the other. *Childhood, 7*, 335–357.

Jahoda, G. (1962). Development of Scottish children's ideas and attitudes about other countries. *Journal of Social Psychology, 58*, 91–108.

Jahoda, G. (1963a). The development of children's ideas about country and nationality, Part I: The conceptual framework. *British Journal of Educational Psychology, 33*, 47–60.

Jahoda, G. (1963b). The development of children's ideas about country and nationality, Part II: National symbols and themes. *British Journal of Educational Psychology, 33*, 143–153.

Jaspers, J. M. F., van de Geer, J. P., Tajfel, H., & Johnson, N. (1972). On the development of national attitudes in children. *European Journal of Social Psychology, 2*, 347–369.

Johnson, N., Middleton, M., & Tajfel, H. (1970). The relationship between children's preferences for and knowledge about other nations. *British Journal of Social and Clinical Psychology, 9*, 232–240.

Lambert, W. E., & Klineberg, O. (1967). *Children's views of foreign peoples: A cross-national study*. New York, NY: Appleton-Century-Crofts.

Maehr, S. (2005). *"How can one be proud? I am not a Nazi!": An investigation of German pupils' sense of national identity and knowledge of national symbols.*. Unpublished BSc dissertation, University of Surrey, UK.

Manouka, A. (2001). *Self-concept and ethnic identity of Albanian children who have emigrated in Greece*. Unpublished MSc dissertation, University of Surrey, UK.

Middleton, M., Tajfel, H., & Johnson, N. (1970). Cognitive and affective aspects of children's national attitudes. *British Journal of Social and Clinical Psychology, 9*, 122–134.

Moodie, M. A. (1980). The development of national identity in White South African schoolchildren. *Journal of Social Psychology, 111*, 169–180.

Moore, S. W., Lare, J., & Wagner, K. A. (1985). *The child's political world: A longitudinal perspective*. New York, NY: Praeger.

Mummendey, A., Kessler, T., Klink, A., & Mielke, R. (1999). Strategies to cope with negative social identity: Predictions by social identity theory and relative deprivation theory. *Journal of Personality and Social Psychology, 76*, 229–245.

Nesdale, D. (2004). Social identity processes and children's ethnic prejudice. In M. Bennett & F. Sani (Eds.), *The development of the social self* (pp. 219–245). Hove, UK: Psychology Press.

Nesdale, D. (2008). Social identity development and children's ethnic attitudes in Australia. In S. M. Quintana & C. McKown (Eds.), *The handbook of race, racism and the developing child* (pp. 313–338). Hoboken, NJ: Wiley.

Oppenheimer, L. (2005). The development of enemy images: Measurement and initial findings. *British Journal of Developmental Psychology, 23*, 645–660.

Oppenheimer, L. (2006). The development of enemy images: A theoretical contribution. *Peace and Conflict: Journal of Peace Psychology, 12*, 269–292.

Oppenheimer, L. (2010). Are children's views of the "enemy" shaped by a highly publicized negative event? *International Journal of Behavioral Development, 34*, 345–353.

Oppenheimer, L., & Hakvoort, I. (2003). Will the Germans ever be forgiven? Memories of the Second World War generations later. In E. Cairns & M. D. Roe (Eds.), *The role of memory in ethnic conflict* (pp. 94–104). Basingstoke, UK: Palgrave-Macmillan.

Penny, R., Barrett, M., & Lyons, E. (2001, August). *Children's naïve theories of nationality: a study of Scottish and English children's national inclusion criteria*. Poster presented at the 10th European Conference on Developmental Psychology, Uppsala University, Uppsala, Sweden.

Piaget, J., & Weil, A. M. (1951). The development in children of the idea of the homeland and of relations to other countries. *International Social Science Journal, 3*, 561–578.

Povrzanović, M. (1997). Children, war and nation: Croatia 1991–4. *Childhood: A Global Journal of Child Research, 4*, 81–102.

Reizábal, L., Valencia, J., & Barrett, M. (2004). National identifications and attitudes to national ingroups and outgroups among children living in the Basque Country. *Infant and Child Development, 13*, 1–20.

Sahlabadi, M. (2002). *The strength of national identity, identity motivations and beliefs about war of Iranian adolescents raised in England and Iran*. Unpublished BSc dissertation, University of Surrey, UK.

Schleicher, K., & Kozma, T. (Eds.). (1992). *Ethnocentrism in education*. Frankfurt, Germany: Peter Lang.

Simon, B. (2004). *Identity in modern society: A social-psychological perspective*. Oxford, UK: Blackwell.

Tajfel, H. (1978). Social categorization, social identity and social comparison. In H. Tajfel (Ed.), *Differentiation between social groups: Studies in the social psychology of intergroup relations* (pp. 61–76). London, UK: Academic Press.

Tajfel, H., Jahoda, G., Nemeth, C., Rim, Y., & Johnson, N. (1972). The devaluation by children of their own national and ethnic group: Two case studies. *British Journal of Social and Clinical Psychology, 11,* 235–243.

Tajfel, H., & Turner, J. C. (1986). The social identity theory of intergroup behaviour. In S. Worchel & W. G. Austin (Eds.), *Psychology of intergroup relations* (2nd ed., pp. 7–24). Chicago, IL: Nelson-Hall.

Takriti, R. (2002). *The development of religious identity in Christian, Hindu and Muslim children.* Unpublished PhD thesis, University of Surrey, UK.

Teichman, Y. (2001). The development of Israeli children's images of Jews and Arabs and their expression in human figure drawings. *Developmental Psychology, 37,* 749–761.

Teichman, Y., & Bar-Tal, D. (2008). Acquisition and development of a shared psychological intergroup repertoire in a context of an intractable conflict. In S. M. Quintana & C. McKown (Eds.), *The handbook of race, racism and the developing child* (pp. 452–482). Hoboken, NJ: Wiley.

Trimby, H. (2005). *The development of Welsh children's sense of national identity.* Unpublished BSc dissertation, University of Surrey, UK.

Vethanayagam, S., & Barrett, M. (2007, September). *English, Indian and Pakistani children's national, ethnic and religious identifications.* Poster presented at the Annual Conference of the Social Psychology Section of the British Psychological Society, University of Kent, UK.

Vila, I., del Valle, A., Perera, S., Monreal, P., & Barrett, M. (1998). Autocategorizacion, identidad nacional y contexto linguistico [Self-categorization, national identity and linguistic context]. *Estudios de Psicologia, 60,* 3–14.

Weinstein, E. A. (1957). Development of the concept of flag and the sense of national identity. *Child Development, 28,* 167–174.

Wiegand, P. (1991a). The "known world" of primary school children. *Geography, 76,* 143–149.

Wiegand, P. (1991b). Does travel broaden the mind? *Education, 3,* 54–58.

EUROPEAN JOURNAL OF DEVELOPMENTAL PSYCHOLOGY
2011, 8 (1), 25–42

Ψ Psychology Press
Taylor & Francis Group

National identifications and attitudes towards a "traditional enemy" nation among English children

Daisy Clay and Martyn Barrett

Department of Psychology, University of Surrey, Guildford, Surrey, UK

This study investigated national identifications and national attitudes among White English children aged 6–7 and 10–11 years old. Eighty children were interviewed using a scale to measure their strength of national identification, and using a trait attribution task and affect questions to measure their attitudes towards four target groups: English people (the in-group), German people (a salient "traditional enemy" out-group), French people (a salient and positively liked out-group) and Dutch people (a non-salient out-group). It was found that the children's attitudes to German people developed differently from the way in which their attitudes to French and Dutch people developed. There was also consistent evidence of in-group favouritism, at both ages. However, there were no significant relationships between the strength of national identification and attitudes towards any of the four target groups, and there were also no gender differences on any of the measures. It is argued that these findings cannot be explained by cognitive-developmental theory. In addition, while social identity theory is able to explain the different developmental patterns displayed by the children's out-group attitudes, this theory has difficulty in explaining the lack of any relationship between the children's national identifications and attitudes It is suggested that English children's national attitudes may be driven more by exogenous sources of information about salient national groups than by social identity processes per se.

Keywords: National identity; National attitudes; Enemy; In-group favouritism.

INTRODUCTION

This study investigated the national identifications of English children, and examined the relationship between these identifications and the children's

Correspondence should be addressed to Martyn Barrett, Department of Psychology, University of Surrey, Guildford, Surrey GU2 7XH, UK. E-mail: m.barrett@surrey.ac.uk

http://www.psypress.com/edp   DOI: 10.1080/17405629.2010.533964

national attitudes. In particular, the study explored whether these children's strength of national identification was related to their attitudes towards a salient and positively evaluated national out-group (French people), a non-salient national out-group (Dutch people) and a salient national out-group, which has been perceived to be the "traditional enemy" of the national in-group for many years (German people).

England presents a complex context in which to examine the relationship between national identifications and attitudes. England is one of the three constituent nations of Great Britain (the other two being Scotland and Wales). Great Britain and Northern Ireland together make up the United Kingdom (UK). England has dominated Great Britain politically, culturally and economically for several centuries, and, as a result, the concept of Britishness has acquired strong Anglocentric connotations (Kumar, 2003). Condor (1996) and Kiely, McCrone, and Bechhofer (2005) found that English people are sometimes confused about the difference between the terms "English" and "British" and may even use them interchangeably. That said, Abell, Condor, Lowe, Gibson, and Stevenson (2007) also found that some English people (e.g., those with extreme right-wing political affiliations) do draw a very clear and explicit distinction between "English" and "British", and construe "English" as a distinctive category, which is directly contrasted with "British", "Scottish" and "Welsh". In addition, for at least some English adults, the identities of "English" and "British" are associated with different conceptual contents: "English" tends to be associated with sport (especially football and cricket), landscapes (green fields and rolling hills), architectural styles (English Gothic and Tudor), and cultural heritage (English stately country homes; Abell et al., 2007; Condor, 2006; Lunn, 1996), whereas "British" is usually associated with the British Empire, the monarchy, foreign policy and ethnic diversity (Condor, 2006; ETHNOS, 2005; Lunn, 1996; Vadher & Barrett, 2009).

A further difference is that the category of "English" is implicitly interpreted by many English people as a racial and/or ethnic category such that members of non-White ethnic-minority groups can never be viewed as English no matter how assimilated they may be in terms of their cultural practices, attitudes and identifications (Abell et al., 2007; Kumar, 2003; Parekh, 2000; Phoenix, 1995). In their turn, ethnic-minority individuals living in England are far less likely to identify with England and Englishness than majority White individuals, and are instead more likely to identify with Britain and Britishness which, unlike England and Englishness, are construed as superordinate and racially and ethnically inclusive (Stone & Muir, 2007; Tilley, Exley, & Heath, 2004; Vadher & Barrett, 2009).

However, the category of "English" is not only defined in contradistinction to "British", "Scottish", "Welsh" and ethnic and racial minority groups; it is also defined in contradistinction to "German" and "French", two salient nations that are in close geographical proximity to England. German people are especially salient to English people, being perceived by many as the "traditional enemy" of England. This perception of Germany is a historical legacy of the two World Wars, a legacy that is regularly resuscitated, perpetuated and promulgated by the English mass media (especially tabloid newspapers) in their reporting of relationships between England and Germany, particularly in the context of football matches between the two countries (Beck, 2006; Downing, 2000; Fedeler, 2008).

Evaluative attitudes towards German people are acquired by English children at a relatively early age, and Germans are the national out-group towards which young English children typically express the least positive attitudes (Barrett, 2007; Barrett & Short, 1992; Barrett, Wilson, & Lyons, 2003; Byram, Esarte-Sarries, & Taylor, 1991; Johnson, 1966, 1973). That said, while English children's attitudes towards Germans are usually significantly less positive than their attitudes towards any other national out-group, German peoples are not always described with predominantly negative characteristics, suggesting that English children tend to hold representations of Germans that are neutral rather than negative overall (see Barrett & Short, 1992; Barrett et al., 2003). Indeed, in a recent study which included English 6-, 9-, 12- and 15-year-olds, Barrett (2007) found that, at all four ages, there were no significant differences in the number of negative and positive attributes ascribed to German people by these children, suggesting a neutral rather than a negative evaluation of German people overall. That said, these same children did ascribe significantly more positive than negative traits to all of the other out-groups that were tested (Spanish, Italian, French and Scottish people) and Germans were a unique exception in not showing this general pattern. A second finding of interest was that there were no changes in the children's overall positivity towards, or affect for, German people with age.

Historically, the French nation has also been a salient European out-group in the evolution of English and British identity, especially during the eighteenth and nineteenth centuries (Kumar, 2003). Today, attitudes to France and to French people are generally very positive within England, and France was the second most popular holiday destination (after Spain) for British people between 2003 and 2007 (Office for National Statistics, 2009). Previous studies that have examined English children's attitudes to French people (Barrett, 2007; Barrett & Short, 1992; Johnson, Middleton, & Tajfel, 1970; Middleton, Tajfel, & Johnson, 1970) have revealed that French people are positively liked, and that overall levels of positivity towards, and liking of, French people typically do not change between 6 and 12 years of age.

In the present study, English children's attitudes towards German, French and Dutch people were examined. To the best of our knowledge, this is the first study to examine English children's attitudes to Dutch people. Like France and Germany, The Netherlands is situated relatively close to England. However, the Dutch are not a salient nation in the construction of English national identity, unlike the Germans and French. Hence, one purpose of the present study was to examine the extent to which the development of attitudes towards salient out-groups (German and French people) is similar to, or different from, the development of attitudes towards a non-salient out-group (Dutch people).

Social identity theory postulates that attitudes towards different out-groups will differ depending upon the salience and relevance of those out-groups for the definition of the in-group (Tajfel & Turner, 1986; Turner, 1999). By contrast, the cognitive-developmental approach to the development of prejudice does not draw any conceptual distinction between attitudes to salient versus non-salient out-groups, but instead postulates that attitudes towards all out-groups become more positive through middle childhood as a consequence of changes to the child's cognitive and sociocognitive understanding (Aboud, 1988; Aboud & Amato, 2001; Doyle & Aboud, 1995). Social identity theory further argues that attitudes to out-groups can also vary according to a number of other factors, including the perceived status of the out-group and the perceived legitimacy and stability of the status differential between the out-group and the in-group (Tajfel & Turner, 1986; Turner, 1999; see also Barrett & Davis, 2008). There is existing evidence that English children's attitudes to German and French people do not change during middle childhood (Barrett, 2007; Barrett & Short, 1992), contrary to the predictions of cognitive-developmental theory. Hence, the present study was designed, in part, to test between these two theories: it was anticipated that support would be found for the predictions of social identity theory rather than cognitive-developmental theory, and that attitudes towards the three out-groups would develop in different ways from each other.

A second issue that was explored in this study was whether the strength of English children's national identifications changes through the course of middle childhood. Much previous research into children's national attitudes has omitted to measure the strength of national identification (e.g., Jahoda, 1962; Lambert & Klineberg, 1967; Middleton et al., 1970; Piaget & Weil, 1951). From the perspective of evaluating the findings of these earlier studies, this may be an unfortunate omission because social-psychological research with adults has revealed that the strength of identification with an in-group can be an important influence on attitudes towards both the in-group and salient comparison out-groups, with there being systematic differences in the attitudes of low and high identifiers (e.g., Jetten, Spears, & Manstead, 2001; Mummendey, Klink, & Brown, 2001; Perreault & Bourhis, 1998; Schmitt & Branscombe, 2001). Hence, in the present study, the strength of English children's national identification was assessed in order to ascertain whether there were any changes in the strength of national identification through the course of middle childhood, at the time when their attitudes to other nations were developing.

Third, this study investigated the relationship between the strength of national identification on the one hand and children's national attitudes on the other. It was anticipated that, if out-groups need to be salient and relevant comparators for the definition of the in-group in order for social identity processes to occur in relationship to those out-groups (as Tajfel & Turner, 1986, proposed in their original formulation of social identity theory; see also Turner, 1999, and Barrett & Oppenheimer, 2011 this issue), then there may not be any relationship between the strength of English national identification and attitudes to Dutch people. However, such a relationship should be present in the cases of attitudes to German and French people, as these are both salient and relevant out-groups for the construction of English national identity. Hence, the present study tested this prediction made by social identity theory, namely that a relationship between national identifications and attitudes would only be present in the cases of attitudes to German and French people. Furthermore, because, on a strict reading, social identity theory may be construed as only predicting relationships between the strength of identification and the magnitude of the discrepancy between attitudes towards the in-group and attitudes towards salient out-groups, this study crucially examined whether there is a relationship between national identification and the positive distinctiveness of the in-group over the out-groups, with relationships only being anticipated in the cases of the German and French out-groups.

A fourth issue that was investigated was whether there are gender differences in English children's national identifications and attitudes. Previous studies have suggested that, among some populations, boys have higher levels of national pride than girls (Amadeo, Torney-Purta, Lehmann, Husfeldt, & Nikolova, 2002; Torney-Purta, Lehmann, Oswald, & Schulz, 2001), and that boys sometimes hold less positive attitudes to other national groups than girls (Byram et al., 1991). However, these findings are by no means universal (see Barrett, 2007, for a review). One possible explanation of these gender differences (where they occur) is that sporting events are a potent arena in which national identifications and attitudes are forged, an explanation that is consistent with findings that sporting figures, events and locations are often elicited when adults (ETHNOS, 2005) and children (Forrest & Barrett, 2001) are asked to produce emblems of their own nation. The fact that boys typically have higher levels of interest in sport than girls (Beal, 1994) may therefore explain these gender differences in national identifications and attitudes, where they occur. An alternative possibility is that boys watch war films and play war games more frequently than girls

(Clifford, Gunter, & McAleer, 1995; Goldstein, 1992, 1994; Valkenburg, 2004), both of which also comprise two potent sites for the constructions of national attitudes. Insofar as English–German rivalry today is primarily flagged by the British mass media in the context of sporting events where metaphorical connections are frequently made to the two World Wars, it was expected that, if gender differences were to be found in the present study, then they would be most likely to occur in the children's attitudes to German people, with boys exhibiting less positive attitudes than girls, and with boys exhibiting higher levels of national identification than girls.

To summarize, this study investigated: (i) whether English children's attitudes towards different national out-groups develop in a similar or varied manner through the course of middle childhood; (ii) whether English children's strength of national identification changes during middle childhood; (iii) whether, among these children, there is a relationship between the strength of English national identification and the positive distinctiveness of English people over German and French people, but not between the strength of English national identification and the positive distinctiveness of English people over Dutch people; and (iv) whether English children display gender differences in their national identifications and attitudes.

METHOD

Participants

A sample of 80 English school children (40 girls and 40 boys) participated in the study. The sample was recruited from two primary schools located in the counties of Surrey and Hampshire in the south-east of England. Because the category of English is racialized, all children were of white English ethnicity. Children were recruited from two age ranges. The younger group consisted of children aged 6–7 years old (mean age = 6.64, $SD = 0.29$), while the older group consisted of children aged 10–11 years old (mean age = 10.64, $SD = 0.32$).

Equal numbers of girls and boys were recruited to each age group. Table 1 shows the mean ages of the children broken down by age group and gender.

TABLE 1
Mean ages of participants, broken down by age and gender
(with standard deviations in parentheses)

	Girls (n = 20)	Boys (n = 20)
Younger	6.65 (0.33)	6.63 (0.26)
Older	10.62 (0.37)	10.67 (0.28)

Procedure

Each child was interviewed separately in a quiet room within their school. After establishing rapport with the child, it was explained that the interviewer was interested in what they thought about certain things and that the child would be asked to complete some tasks and answer some questions. Each child was reassured that they were not being tested, that there were no good or bad answers, and that no one other than the interviewer would know what they had said.

Three tasks were then administered to the child. The first task consisted of the six questions comprising the National Identification scale, in which the term English was used to denote the national identity being tested; the second task consisted of the trait attribution task in which the child was asked to select, from a set of six positive and six negative traits, those traits which applied to English people, German people, French people and Dutch people (with each target group being tested independently from the other groups); the third task consisted of a pair of questions designed to assess the child's general liking of/affect towards each of the four target groups on a 5-point rating scale running from *like a lot* to *dislike a lot*. For full details of all three tasks and the randomization procedures that were employed in their administration, see Barrett and Oppenheimer (2011 this issue).

RESULTS

Data screening and preparation

The scores obtained from the six questions used to measure the children's national identifications were subjected to an exploratory principal components analysis using varimax rotation. This revealed that all six items loaded onto a single factor (eigenvalue $= 2.78$; percentage of variance explained $= 46.37\%$), with the loadings of the items on this factor ranging between .52 and .76. The six items also scaled reliably (Cronbach's alpha $= .81$). Because responses to the questions were scored using a mixture of 4- and 5-point scales, the responses scored on the 4-point scales were rescored onto 5-point scales, and the scores on all six questions were then averaged in order to derive a mean strength of national identification score (NI; scores ranging between 1 and 5).

On the trait attribution task, the total number of positive traits (PT; scores ranging from 0–6), the total number of negative traits (NT; scores ranging from 0–6), and an overall positivity score obtained by subtracting the number of negative traits from the number of positive traits (POS; scores ranging from -6 to $+6$) were calculated for each of the four target groups individually. In addition, the positive distinctiveness attributed to English people over each of the three out-groups individually was calculated by subtracting each of the three out-group POS scores from the English in-group POS score in turn (PD; scores ranging between -12 and $+12$).

The scores from the general affect (liking) questions were analysed as they stood (AFF; scores ranging from 1–5). In addition, the affective distinctiveness of English people over each of the three out-groups individually was calculated by subtracting each of the three out-group AFF scores from the English in-group AFF score in turn (AD; scores ranging between -4 and $+4$).

In the analyses reported below, only the statistically significant results are reported. All other results were non-significant.

National identification scores

The NI scores were analysed using a 2 (Age Group) $\times$ 2 (Gender) between-groups analysis of variance (ANOVA), which only showed a significant main effect of age group, $F(1, 76) = 5.94$, $p < .05$. National identification was stronger among the younger children ($M = 4.42$, $SD = 0.64$) than the older children ($M = 4.11$, $SD = 0.49$).

Scores derived from the trait attribution task

The PT and NT scores were analysed using a 2 (Age Group) $\times$ 2 (Gender) $\times$ 2 (PT vs. NT) $\times$ 4 (Target Group: English, German, French, Dutch) mixed ANOVA, with independent groups on the first two factors and repeated measures on the last two factors. This revealed a significant main effect of Target Group, $F(3, 59) = 8.13$, $p < .001$, a significant main effect of PT vs. NT, $F(1, 61) = 105.52$, $p < .001$, a significant main effect of Age Group, $F(1, 61) = 9.59$, $p < .005$, a significant interaction between Target Group and PT vs. NT, $F(3, 59) = 15.06$, $p < .001$, and a significant three-way interaction between Target Group, PT vs. NT and Age Group, $F(3, 59) = 3.02$, $p < .05$.

Post hoc ANOVAs and t-tests were conducted to locate where these effects were occurring. These revealed that significantly more positive traits were assigned to English people ($M = 4.19$, $SD = 1.47$) than to French ($M = 3.53$, $SD = 1.67$), Dutch ($M = 3.01$, $SD = 1.67$) and German ($M = 2.64$, $SD = 1.90$) people, and that significantly more positive traits were assigned to French people than to Dutch and German people. In addition, significantly more negative traits were assigned to German people ($M = 1.84$, $SD = 1.54$) than to English people ($M = 1.04$, $SD = 1.40$), French people ($M = 1.07$, $SD = 1.42$) and Dutch people ($M = 1.35$, $SD = 1.67$). The main effect of PT vs. NT was due to more positive traits than negative traits being assigned to all four groups (see preceding means). The main effect of

Age Group was due to the younger children assigning more positive traits and more negative traits overall than the older children (see Table 2 for means).

The two-way interaction between Target Group and PT vs. NT was qualified by the three-way interaction between Target Group, PT vs. NT and Age Group. The relevant means are shown in Table 2. Post hoc analyses revealed that the English PT and NT scores did not differ as a function of age, the French and Dutch NT scores (but not the French and Dutch PT scores) were significantly lower in the older children than in the younger children, while the German PT scores (but not the German NT scores) were significantly lower in the older children than in the younger children. In other words, the pattern of age differences in relationship to the three out-groups was different depending upon whether the target group was the "traditional enemy" out-group or another kind of out-group.

Next, the overall positivity (POS) scores for each of the four target groups were analysed using a 2 (Age Group) × 2 (Gender) × 4 (Target Group: English, German, French, Dutch) mixed ANOVA, with independent groups on the first two factors and repeated measures on the last factor. This revealed only a significant main effect of Target Group, $F(3, 183) = 18.46$, $p < .001$. Post hoc t-tests revealed that all four means were significantly different from each other (English $M = 3.05$, $SD = 1.94$; French $M = 2.52$, $SD = 2.30$; Dutch $M = 1.69$, $SD = 2.26$; German $M = 0.81$, $SD = 2.51$). One-sample t-tests further showed that all four means were significantly higher than 0, indicating that attitudes to all four national groups were positive overall, including attitudes to Germans; German $t(72) = 2.75$, $p < .01$.

The three positive distinctiveness (PD) scores were also analysed using a 2 (Age Group) × 2 (Gender) × 3 (PD Score: English–German, English–

TABLE 2

Mean number of positive traits (PT) and negative traits (NT) assigned to each of the four target groups, broken down by age (with standard deviations in parentheses)

	PT		NT	
Target group	Younger	Older	Younger	Older
English	4.30[1] (1.38)	3.93[1] (1.53)	1.20[1] (1.65)	0.93[1] (1.21)
German	**3.31[2,3] (1.90)**	**2.00[2] (1.70)**	2.03[2] (1.78)	1.65[2] (1.25)
French	3.78[2] (1.84)	3.30[3] (1.49)	**1.36[1,3] (1.69)**	**0.68[1] (0.97)**
Dutch	3.16[3] (1.90)	2.89[4] (1.47)	**1.90[2,3] (1.83)**	**0.83[1] (1.34)**

Notes: The location of significant differences within columns are shown using superscript numbers, with mean scores which do not differ significantly from one another sharing the same superscript number. Within the PT and NT columns, pairs of cells that are significantly different from each other are shown in **bold**.

French, English–Dutch) mixed ANOVA, with independent groups on the first two factors and repeated measures on the last factor. This revealed a significant main effect of PD Score, $F(2, 122) = 13.24$, $p < .001$, and a significant interaction between PD Score and Age Group, $F(2, 122) = 3.17$, $p < .05$. The relevant means are shown in Table 3.

Post hoc t-tests revealed that the three overall PD scores were all significantly different from each other. However, among the younger children, the English–German and the English–Dutch PD scores did not differ significantly from each other but both were significantly different from the English–French PD scores. By contrast, among the older children, the English–French and the English–Dutch PD scores did not differ significantly from each other but both were significantly different from the English–German PD scores. As the figures in Table 3 show, with increasing age, the positive distinctiveness of the in-group over the "traditional enemy" out-group increased, while the positive distinctiveness of the in-group over the other two out-groups decreased.

Scores derived from the affect questions

The affect (AFF) scores were analysed using a 2 (Age Group) × 2 (Gender) × 4 (Target Group: English, German, French, Dutch) mixed ANOVA, with independent groups on the first two factors and repeated measures on the last factor. This only revealed a significant main effect of Target Group, $F(3, 66) = 38.50$, $p < .001$.

Post hoc t-tests indicated that affect was significantly higher towards English people ($M = 4.68$, $SD = 0.62$) than to French ($M = 3.85$, $SD = 0.97$), German ($M = 3.25$, $SD = 1.32$) and Dutch ($M = 3.19$, $SD = 1.15$) people, and that affect was also significantly higher towards French people than to German and Dutch people. However, affect towards German and Dutch people did not differ significantly. One-sample t-tests further revealed that while affect towards both English people, $t(75) = 23.85$, $p < .001$, and

TABLE 3
Mean positive distinctiveness (PD) scores, broken down by age (with standard deviations in parentheses)

PD score	Younger	Older	Overall
English–German	1.93[1] (2.64)	2.66[1] (2.91)	2.32[1] (2.79)
English–French	0.70[2] (2.74)	0.46[2] (2.34)	0.57[2] (2.52)
English–Dutch	2.03[1] (2.53)	1.06[2] (2.61)	1.51[3] (2.60)

Notes: The location of significant differences within columns are shown using superscript numbers, with mean scores which do not differ significantly from one another sharing the same superscript number.

French people, $t(77) = 7.72$, $p < .001$, was significantly higher than the neutral mid-point of the affect scale (3), affect towards German people and Dutch people was not significantly higher than the neutral midpoint.

The affective distinctiveness (AD) scores were then analysed using a 2 (Age Group) × 2 (Gender) × 3 (AD Score: English–German, English–French, English–Dutch) mixed ANOVA, with independent groups on the first two factors and repeated measures on the last factor. This also only revealed a significant main effect of AD Score, $F(2, 136) = 9.48$, $p < .001$. Post hoc t-tests showed that English–German AD ($M = 1.39$, $SD = 1.51$) and English–Dutch AD ($M = 1.49$, $SD = 1.26$) did not differ, but both were significantly larger than English–French AD ($M = 0.81$, $SD = 1.07$).

The correlations between the variables

Finally, all of the measures were correlated with each other, controlling for age. The results are shown in Table 4. Some of the significant correlations were expected (due to the non-independence of the measures involved), particularly those between the PT and NT scores on the one hand and the corresponding POS and PD scores on the other hand. Similarly, the significant correlations between the AFF scores and the corresponding AD scores were also expected.

More interestingly, the following patterns are apparent from Table 4. First, there were no significant correlations between the NI scores and any of the attitudinal measures. Second, affect towards English people (AFFEng) did not correlate significantly with any other measures (except with the three AD scores, which can be disregarded as the AFFEng and AD scores were non-independent). Third, all of the PT scores for the four target groups were significantly correlated with each other (and four out of the six pairs of NT scores were significantly correlated with each other as well). This suggests that children's attitudes to national groups are structured in such a way that if they are positive towards one group, they are positive to all groups. Fourth, the PT and NT scores for the two salient out-groups (German, French) were systematically related to the AFF scores for those out-groups; however, this relationship was not present in the case of the in-group (English) nor in the case of the non-salient out-group (Dutch).

DISCUSSION

This study was designed to investigate four main research questions. The first question was whether English children's attitudes towards different national out-groups develop in a similar or varied manner through the course of middle childhood. The study found differences in the development of attitudes to the three out-groups. For example, the children's attitudes to

TABLE 4
Partial correlations between all of the measures, controlling for age

	PTEng	NTEng	PTGer	NTGer	PTFre	NTFre	PTDut	NTDut	POSEng	POSGer	POSFre	POSDut	PDGer	PDFre	PDDut	AFFEng	AFFGer	AFFFre	AFFDut	ADGer	ADFre	ADDut
NI	.15	.10	−.05	.09	.03	.07	−.04	−.08	.04	−.09	−.02	.03	.11	.05	.00	.25	.03	.14	.07	.06	−.01	.03
PTEng		.01	.31*	.53***	−.03	.45***	−.11	.72***	.31*	.38**	.40**	.18	.18	.18	.15	.23	.16	.21	.08	−.07	−.09	.01
NTEng			.28*	.32*	.24	.51***	.14	.21	−.69***	.00	−.11	−.04	−.45***	−.42***	−.48***	.00	−.07	.00	−.01	.07	.00	.01
PTGer				−.23	.41**	.05	.57***	−.08	.03	.82***	.26	.47***	−.73***	−.23	−.43***	.06	.49***	−.10	.21	−.43***	.12	−.18
NTGer					−.18	.48***	−.10	.55***	−.34***	−.75***	−.39**	−.44***	.47***	.11	.16	.03	−.50***	−.03	−.13	.46***	.05	.13
PTFre						−.30*	.44***	.04	−.10	.38**	.85***	.29*	−.21	−.66***	−.12	.14	.18	.40**	−.13	−.12	−.31*	.17
NTFre							−.05	.06	−.37***	−.25	−.75***	−.08	−.01	.44***	−.21	−.03	−.23	−.36**	.08	.19	.33*	−.09
PTDut								−.02	.23	.44***	.33*	.75***	−.26	−.14	−.54***	.13	.41**	−.04	.26	−.33**	.09	−.19
NTDut									−.23	−.39**	.00	−.68***	.45***	−.17	.47***	−.14	−.31*	.09	−.19	.23	−.15	.12
POSEng										.22	.35*	.32*	−.14	.43***	.44***	.17	.17	.15	.06	−.10	−.07	.01
POSGer											.40**	.58***	−.77***	−.22	−.39**	.02	.63***	−.05	.22	−.56***	.05	−.20
POSFre												.24	−.22	−.70***	.03	.11	.25	.47***	−.13	−.19	−.39**	.16
POSDut													−.39**	.01	−.71***	.19	.51***	−.09	.32*	−.39**	.17	−.22
PDGer														.50***	.64***	.09	−.47***	.14	−.16	.45***	−.09	.19
PDFre															.31*	.02	−.11	−.34*	.17	.11	.33*	−.15
PDDut																−.06	−.36*	.20	−.25	.30*	−.21	.21
AFFEng																	−.14	.15	.20	.45***	.36**	.37***
AFFGer																		.15	.11	−.95***	−.20	−.49***
AFFFre																			.12	−.09	−.88***	−.07
AFFDut																				−.42***	.11	−.92***
ADGer																					.30*	.56***
ADFre																						.23

Notes: NI = Strength of English national identification; PTEng = Positive traits to English; NTEng = Negative traits to English; PTGer = Positive traits to Germans; NTGer = Negative traits to Germans; PTFre = Positive traits to French; NTFre = Negative traits to French; PTDut = Positive traits to Dutch; NTDut = Negative traits to Dutch; POSEng = Overall positivity to English; POSGer = Overall positivity to Germans; POSFre = Overall positivity to French; POSDut = Overall positivity to Dutch; PDGer = Positive distinctiveness of English over Germans; PDFre = Positive distinctiveness of English over French; PDDut = Positive distinctiveness of English over Dutch; AFFEng = Affect for English; AFFGer = Affect for Germans; AFFFre = Affect for French; AFFDut = Affect for Dutch; ADGer = Affective distinctiveness of English over Germans; ADFre = Affective distinctiveness of English over French; ADDut = Affective distinctiveness of English over Dutch. *$p < .05$; **$p < .005$; ***$p < .001$.

French people were more positive than their attitudes to both Dutch and German people (e.g., as indexed by both positive trait attributions and affect). However, while on some measures the children's attitudes to Dutch and German people were not significantly different (e.g., on the positive trait attributions and on affect), the children's attitudes to Dutch people developed in a similar way to their attitudes to French people (with the number of negative traits ascribed to these two groups decreasing with age), while their attitudes to German people displayed a different developmental pattern (in which the number of positive traits ascribed to Germans decreased with age: see Table 2). It was also found that the positive distinctiveness of English people over German people became more pronounced with age, while the positive distinctiveness of English people over the other two out-groups showed the opposite pattern (see Table 3). However, while affect towards French people was significantly higher than the neutral mid-point of the affect scale, affect towards both German and Dutch people was not significantly higher than the neutral mid-point of the scale.

This differentiated pattern in the development of attitudes towards out-groups suggests that the cognitive-developmental explanation of the development of prejudice (Aboud, 1988; Aboud & Amato, 2001), according to which attitudes towards all out-groups become more positive through middle childhood as a consequence of developmental shifts in the child's sociocognitive understanding of large-scale social groups, is inadequate, as it fails to explain why attitudes to different out-groups develop in these different ways. Cognitive-developmental theory also fails to explain why, in the present study, the number of positive traits ascribed to Germans actually decreased, rather than increased, with age: this trend is in direct contradiction to the predictions of cognitive-developmental theory (Doyle & Aboud, 1995; Doyle, Beaudet, & Aboud, 1988).

By contrast, social identity theory (Tajfel & Turner, 1986; Turner 1999), which postulates that intergroup attitudes are influenced by a number of factors (including the salience of the out-group concerned and its relevance for the definition of the in-group, and the status of the out-group in relationship to the in-group) is able to account for the differentiated patterns of attitudes to the different out-groups. Indeed, social identity theory can readily explain the differences displayed in the development of attitudes to German people versus French and Dutch people: older children are more likely than younger children to have knowledge of the historical intergroup relationships that have existed between England and Germany; hence, differences in attitudes towards German people versus the other two out-groups are more likely to be displayed by the older children than the younger children (the pattern which was indeed found in this study).

The second research question that was addressed by this study was whether English children's strength of national identification changes during middle childhood. It was found that the strength of national identification decreased significantly between 6–7 and 10–11 years of age. That said, it should be noted that national identification was still very strong, even at the age of 10–11: on a 5-point scale, the mean strength of identification at 10–11 years was 4.11. It is also important to note that this study yielded evidence of in-group favouritism, with the children at both ages showing significantly greater positivity towards the in-group on several measures (e.g., on the number of positive traits attributed to English people, on overall positivity, and on affect for members of the in-group). Hence, care needs to be taken in not overplaying this reduction in the strength of national identification between these two ages. However, one possible explanation of this reduction is that, by the age of 10–11, other identities are increasing in salience for the child as he or she begins to embark on a more extensive exploration of self (Kroger, 2004; Marcia, 1980), and it may be the competition from these other identities that is responsible for the reduction in the strength of national identification at the threshold of adolescence.

The third research question that this study sought to address was whether there is a relationship between the strength of national identification and the positive distinctiveness of the in-group over salient comparison out-groups. The outcome of the correlational analysis was consistent and clear on this issue: there was no relationship between the strength of national identification and any of the attitudinal measures. From the perspective of social identity theory and research with adults, which has shown that there are widespread differences in the attitudes of high and low identifiers (e.g., Jetten et al., 2001; Mummendey et al., 2001; Perreault & Bourhis, 1998; Schmitt & Branscombe, 2001), this outcome is surprising. It suggests that identification with the national in-group is not a dominant factor in driving the development of children's national attitudes, at least not among English children. It is pertinent to note that that this finding is consistent with previous findings reported by Barrett (2007), who similarly failed to find any consistent relationship between national identifications and national attitudes in 6-, 9-, 12- and 15-year-old English children. The issue of the age at which, and how and why, national identifications become a significant predictor of national attitudes among English people remains an open question for future research involving older children and young adults to address. However, one distinct possibility is that children's attitudes towards other national groups are driven neither by their endogenous cognitive-development, nor by social identity processes, but by external sources of information, including holidays in other countries, school teaching and school textbooks, representations in the mass media and peer-group discourse. One of the available theories of how children's national and ethnic identifications and attitudes develop, namely societal-social-cognitive-motivational theory (Barrett, 2007, 2009; Barrett & Davis, 2008; see Barrett & Oppenheimer, 2011 this issue), proposes that all of these factors, as well as cognitive development and social identity processes, can play a role in the development of intergroup attitudes. The evidence from the present study suggests that this kind of conceptual framework may indeed be required if we are to explain all of the different patterns of development and their associated casual factors which have now been documented within different national and sociohistorical contexts.

Fourth, and finally, this research also sought to examine whether English children display gender differences in their national identifications and attitudes. Once again, the study yielded clear and unambiguous findings: no gender differences emerged in any of the analyses that were conducted. Hence, this study adds support for the note of caution expressed by Barrett (2007) concerning the lack of consistency concerning gender differences in children's national identifications and attitudes: gender differences are indeed far from universal in this domain.

In addition to these four principal outcomes, a number of incidental findings were also obtained in this study. For example, it was found that the attributions of positive and negative traits to different national groups were intercorrelated. This suggests that children who feel positively toward their own national group also feel positively toward other national out-groups, while children who feel more negatively about their national in-group feel more negatively about other national groups. It was also found that trait attributions to salient national out-groups correlate with affect towards those out-groups, but the same relationship does not apply in the case of non-salient out-groups or the in-group. This latter finding provides further evidence that children's attitudes towards out-groups are differentiated rather than uniform.

It should be acknowledged that there are limitations to the present study. First, the sample size was relatively small, with only 80 children being tested in total. Second, it would have been useful to test additional children at other ages, particularly through the years of adolescence, in order to ascertain when the relationship between national identifications and national attitudes is established. Third, the measures which were used in this study were global and quantitative in nature. They precluded obtaining more fine-grained information about the children's understanding of national groups and their own national identifications. Future studies would benefit from including qualitative open-ended questions to explore in greater detail children's own subjective perspectives on these issues.

In conclusion, this study has shown that children's attitudes to national out-groups are differentiated. Depending upon the particular out-group concerned, children's attitudes display different developmental patterns. In particular, in the case of English children, attitudes to German people (the "traditional enemy" nation) were found to develop differently from their attitudes to a positively liked out-group (French people) and their attitudes to a non-salient national out-group (Dutch people). These findings cannot be readily explained by cognitive-developmental theory, but can be explained by social identity theory. That said, social identity theory has difficulty in explaining the further finding obtained in this study that national identifications and national attitudes are not related in English children. It is possible that a more comprehensive model such as societal-social-cognitive-motivational theory is required in order to explain the present findings.

REFERENCES

Abell, J., Condor, S., Lowe, R. D., Gibson, S., & Stevenson, C. (2007). Who ate all the pride? Patriotic sentiment and English national football support. *Nations and Nationalism, 13,* 97–116.

Aboud, F. E. (1988). *Children and prejudice.* Oxford, UK: Blackwell.

Aboud, F. E., & Amato, M. (2001). Developmental and socialization influences on intergroup bias. In R. Brown & S. L. Gaertner (Eds.), *Blackwell handbook of social psychology: Intergroup processes* (pp. 65–85). Oxford, UK: Blackwell.

Amadeo, J., Torney-Purta, J., Lehmann, R., Husfeldt, V., & Nikolova, R. (2002). *Civic knowledge and engagement: An IEA study of upper secondary students in sixteen countries.* Amsterdam, The Netherlands: IEA.

Barrett, M. (2007). *Children's knowledge, beliefs and feelings about nations and national groups.* Hove, UK: Psychology Press.

Barrett, M. (2009). The development of children's intergroup attitudes. In A. Hu & M. Byram (Eds.), *Interkulturelle Kompetenz und Fremdsprachliches Lernen: Modelle, Empirie, Evaluation* [Intercultural Competence and Foreign Language Learning: Models, Empiricism, Assessment] (pp. 69–86). Tübingen, Germany: Gunter Narr Verlag.

Barrett, M., & Davis, S. C. (2008). Applying social identity and self-categorization theories to children's racial, ethnic, national and state identifications and attitudes. In S. M. Quintana & C. McKown (Eds.), *The handbook of race, racism and the developing child* (pp. 72–110). Hoboken, NJ: Wiley.

Barret, M., & Oppenheimer, L. (2011). Findings, theories and methods in the study of children's national identification and national attitudes. *European Journal of Development Psychology, 8,* 5–24.

Barrett, M., & Short, J. (1992). Images of European people in a group of 5–10 year old English school children. *British Journal of Developmental Psychology, 10,* 339–363.

Barrett, M., Wilson, H., & Lyons, E. (2003). The development of national in-group bias: English children's attributions of characteristics to English, American and German people. *British Journal of Developmental Psychology, 21,* 193–220.

Beal, C. R. (1994). *Boys and girls: The development of gender roles.* New York, NY: McGraw-Hill.

Beck, P. (2006). Two world wars and one world cup. *BBC History, 7,* 35–39.

Byram, M., Esarte-Sarries, V., & Taylor, S. (1991). *Cultural studies and language learning: A research report.* Clevedon, UK: Multilingual Matters.

Clifford, B. R., Gunter, B., & McAleer, J. (1995). *Television and children: Programme evaluation, comprehension, and impact.* Hove, UK: Lawrence Erlbaum Associates, Ltd.

Condor, S. (1996). Unimagined community? Some social psychological issues concerning English national identity. In G. M. Breakwell & E. Lyons (Eds.), *Changing European identities: Social psychological analyses of social change* (pp. 41–68). Oxford, UK: Butterworth-Heinemann.

Condor, S. (2006). Temporality and collectivity: Diversity, history and the rhetorical construction of national entitativity. *British Journal of Social Psychology, 45*, 657–682.

Downing, D. (2000). *The best of enemies: England v Germany*. London, UK: Bloomsbury.

Doyle, A. B., & Aboud, F. E. (1995). A longitudinal study of White children's racial prejudice as a social-cognitive development. *Merrill-Palmer Quarterly, 41*, 209–228.

Doyle, A. B., Beaudet, J., & Aboud, F. E. (1988). Developmental patterns in the flexibility of children's ethnic attitudes. *Journal of Cross-Cultural Psychology, 19*, 3–18.

ETHNOS. (2005). *Citizenship and belonging: What is Britishness?* London, UK: ETHNOS Research and Consultancy.

Fedeler, A. (2008). *England versus Germany: On Tommies, Krauts and footie foes*. Unpublished Masters Thesis, University of Bergen, Norway.

Forrest, L., & Barrett, M. (2001). *English adolescents' sense of national identity, identity motivations and national historical icons*. Unpublished paper, Department of Psychology, University of Surrey, UK.

Goldstein, J. (1992). Sex differences in aggressive play and toy preference. In K. Björkqvist & P. Niemalä (Eds.), *Of mice and women: Aspects of female aggression* (pp. 65–76). San Diego, CA: Academic Press.

Goldstein, J. H. (Ed.). (1994). *Toys, play, and child development*. Cambridge, UK: Cambridge University Press.

Jahoda, G. (1962). Development of Scottish children's ideas and attitudes about other countries. *Journal of Social Psychology, 58*, 91–108.

Jetten, J., Spears, R., & Manstead, A. S. R. (2001). Similarity as a source of differentiation: The role of group identification. *European Journal of Social Psychology, 31*, 621–640.

Johnson, N. (1966). What do children learn from war comics? *New Society, 8*, 7–12.

Johnson, N. (1973). Development of English children's concept of Germany. *Journal of Social Psychology, 90*, 259–267.

Johnson, N., Middleton, M., & Tajfel, H. (1970). The relationship between children's preferences for and knowledge about other nations. *British Journal of Social and Clinical Psychology, 9*, 232–240.

Kiely, R., McCrone, D., & Bechhofer, F. (2005). Whither Britishness? English and Scottish people in Scotland. *Nations and Nationalism, 11*, 65–82.

Kroger, J. (2004). *Identity in adolescence: The balance between self and other* (3rd ed.). London, UK: Routledge.

Kumar, K. (2003). *The making of English national identity*. Cambridge, UK: Cambridge University Press.

Lambert, W. E., & Klineberg, O. (1967). *Children's views of foreign peoples: A cross-national study*. New York, NY: Appleton-Century-Crofts.

Lunn, K. (1996). Reconsidering "Britishness": The construction and significance of national identity in twentieth-century Britain. In B. Jenkins & S. A. Sofos (Eds.), *National identity in contemporary Europe* (pp. 83–100). London, UK: Routledge.

Marcia, J. (1980). Identity in adolescence. In J. Adelson (Ed.), *Handbook of adolescent psychology* (pp. 159–187). New York, NY: Wiley.

Middleton, M., Tajfel, H., & Johnson, N. (1970). Cognitive and affective aspects of children's national attitudes. *British Journal of Social and Clinical Psychology, 9*, 122–134.

Mummendey, A., Klink, A., & Brown, R. (2001). Nationalism and patriotism: National identification and out-group rejection. *British Journal of Social Psychology, 40*, 159–172.

Office for National Statistics. (2009). *Travel trends 2007: Data and commentary from the 2007 International Passenger Survey*. London, UK: HMSO.

Parekh, B. (2000). *The future of multi-ethnic Britain: The Parekh report*. London, UK: The Runnymede Trust/Profile Books.

Perreault, S., & Bourhis, R. Y. (1998). Social identification, interdependence and discrimination. *Group Processes and Intergroup Relations, 1*, 49–66.

Phoenix, A. (1995). The national identities of young Londoners. *Gulliver, 37*, 86–110.

Piaget, J., & Weil, A. M. (1951). The development in children of the idea of the homeland and of relations to other countries. *International Social Science Journal, 3*, 561–578.

Schmitt, M. T., & Branscombe, N. R. (2001). The good, the bad, and the manly: Threats to one's prototypicality and evaluations of fellow in-group members. *Journal of Experimental Social Psychology, 37*, 510–517.

Stone, L., & Muir, R. (2007). *Who are we? Identities in Britain, 2007*. London, UK: Institute for Public Policy Research (IPPR).

Tajfel, H., & Turner, J. C. (1986). The social identity theory of intergroup behaviour. In S. Worchel & W. G. Austin (Eds.), *Psychology of intergroup relations* (2nd ed., pp. 7–24). Chicago, IL: Nelson-Hall.

Tilley, J., Exley, S. R., & Heath, A. (2004). Dimensions of British identity. In A. Park, J. Curtice, K. Thomson, C. Bromley, & M. Phillips (Eds.), *British social attitudes: The 21st report* (pp. 147–167). London, UK: Sage.

Torney-Purta, J., Lehmann, R., Oswald, H., & Schulz, W. (2001). *Citizenship and education in twenty-eight countries: Civic knowledge and engagement at age fourteen*. Amsterdam, The Netherlands: IEA.

Turner, J. C. (1999). Some current issues in research on social identity and self-categorization theories. In N. Ellemers, R. Spears, & B. Doosje (Eds.), *Social identity* (pp. 6–34). Oxford, UK: Blackwell.

Vadher, K., & Barrett, M. (2009). Boundaries of Britishness in British Indian and Pakistani young adults. *Journal of Community and Applied Social Psychology, 19*, 442–458.

Valkenburg, P. M. (2004). *Children's responses to the screen*. Mahwah, NJ: Lawrence Erlbaum Associates, Inc.

EUROPEAN JOURNAL OF DEVELOPMENTAL PSYCHOLOGY
2011, 8 (1), 43–57

Psychology Press
Taylor & Francis Group

National identification and in-group/out-group attitudes with Bosniak and Serbian children in Bosnia[1]

Louis Oppenheimer and Emina Midzic

Department of Developmental Psychology, University of Amsterdam, Amsterdam, The Netherlands

The purpose of the present study was to examine the relationship between national identity and in-group/out-group attitudes with Bosniak and Serbian children living in Bosnia. In total, 89 Bosniak ($n = 49$) and Serbian ($n = 40$) children aged 7 and 11 years participated in the study. They were presented with the national identity and the in-group/out-group attitudes scale. The data show that the older children attached less importance to their national identity than the younger children. On three out of six scales, Serbian children attributed greater importance to national identity than Bosniak children did. In addition, Bosniak as well as Serbian children attributed more positive characteristics to their own in-group than to the out-groups. They also ascribed more negative adjectives to the out-groups than the in-group. There were no effects for age. The findings show that the relationship between in-group favouritism and out-group derogation is present with Bosniak but not with Serbian children.

Keywords: National identification; In-group/out-group attitudes; Conflict; Bosnian-Bosniak and Bosnian-Serbian children.

Sarajevo, having been a city under attack from 1992 until 1995 and with a history of ethnic and religious diversity, offers an excellent setting in which to study national identity and in-group/out-group attitudes and their

Correspondence should be addressed to Louis Oppenheimer, Department of Psychology, University of Amsterdam, Roetersstraat 15, NL-1018 WB Amsterdam, The Netherlands. E-mail: l.j.t.oppenheimer@uva.nl

[1]The population of Bosnia is a mixture of Muslim Bosniaks, Roman Catholic Croats, Russian Orthodox Serbs, and some other smaller ethnic groups who are all called Bosnians. In this paper, we will talk about Bosnian-Bosniak and Bosnian-Serbian children to differentiate between children belonging to the Bosniak and Serbian population groups in Bosnia.

© 2011 Psychology Press, an imprint of the Taylor & Francis Group, an Informa business

http://www.psypress.com/edp   DOI: 10.1080/17405629.2010.533974

interrelationships. In the present study, we examined the role of national identification with Bosnian-Bosniak and Bosnian-Serbian children aged 7 and 11 in their attitudes toward their own in-group and two out-groups. In fact, this study functioned as a pilot study for the other studies that are reported in this special issue.

The ethnic and religious mixture of Muslim Bosniaks, Roman Catholic Croats, and Russian Orthodox Serbs had co-existed in relative peace in the former Republic of Yugoslavia under the reign of Communist leader Marshal Tito (1892–1980; Garrod et al., 2003). While at that time the different ethnic identities existing in Yugoslavia were acknowledged by the Communist government, they were also severely curbed in their expressions because ethnic identities were perceived as a threat by the Communist political ideology. Following the death of Tito, ethnic nationalism began to rise again in Yugoslavia. Consequently, the Yugoslav Government tried to promote a national Yugoslav identity by the means of public and national rituals in the media, the educational system, and obligatory military service. But because the country was ethnically diverse, it represented a setting full of possibilities for the creation not just of negative images of others but simultaneously also of images of threat (Povrzanovic, 1997). Beginning with Croatia's attempts to secede from the republic of Yugoslavia in 1991, the role of xenophobia and ethnic hatred in the collapse of Yugoslavia became evident. Both the Croat and Serb sides spread fear of both sides in their propaganda by claiming that the other side would engage in oppression and would make use of genocide to increase support from their own populations.

After many decades of co-existence in Communist Yugoslavia and in spite of the absence of any clear-cut territorial boundaries, objective cultural features were still present that differentiated between Croats, Serbs, and Bosniaks. Even when the political situation became explosive, only a few individuals refused to be identified according to their ethnic background.

In 1991, the provinces of Slovenia and Croatia declared independence. Serbia being increasingly controlled by its president Slobodan Milosevic and the Yugoslav Army, which was dominated by Serbian officers, declared war on the then independent republic of Croatia in late 1991. In 1992 Bosnia-Herzegovina governed by a majority of Muslim members of parliament in Sarajevo also declared independence resulting in a revolt of the Serbian population and civil war in which the Serbians in Herzegovina were supported by the military forces of Serbia under the command of Milosevic (Garrod et al., 2003).

During these years, the Bosnian capital Sarajevo was shelled by Serbian forces for 44 months, causing tremendous physical and psychological damage. By means of the peace agreement of Dayton in 1995, peace throughout Bosnia-Herzegovina was achieved. However, as a result the country was divided into two areas, the Muslim-Croatian federation and the Serbian Republic of Srspka. Hence, even today Bosnia-Herzegovina is characterized by political and ethnic divisions.

With this historical background in mind, we studied the role of strength of national identification with Bosnian-Bosniak and Bosnian-Serbian children aged 7 and 11 in their attitudes toward their own in-group and two out-groups. The out-groups consisted of the traditional enemy (i.e., for the Bosnian-Bosniak participants Serbia and for the Bosniak-Serbian participants Bosnia-Herzegovina) and a more neutral country Croatia.

Based on the general expectations of a relationship between strength of national identification and attitudes about the in- and out-group we expected that: (i) children would rate the in-group more positively than the out-groups (Augoustinos & Rosewarne, 2001; Barrett, 1996; Barrett, Wilson, & Lyons, 2003; Bennett, Lyons, Sani, & Barrett, 1998); (ii) that older children (i.e., from age 10 onwards) would rate the in-group more positively than younger children (Augoustinos & Rosewarne, 2001; Barrett, 1996; Barrett et al., 2003; Bar-Tal, 1996; Bennett et al., 1998; and Rutland, 1999, who reported that young adolescents are more sensitive to in-group favouritism and stereotyping than younger children); and (iii) because the present study was conducted in a setting that had recently experienced armed conflict and the participating children were from two different ethnic backgrounds that fought each other in the war, we assumed that the greater the strength of national identification, the more positive attitudes toward the in-group and the more negative attitudes toward the out-groups would be. However, because the conflict in the Balkans can be perceived as an example of an intractable conflict (Bar-On, 2006; Bar-Tal, 2010; Teichman & Bar-Tal, 2008), the findings could show an increase in in-group preferences and out-group derogation with the children participating in this study. In addition, it might be expected that such processes would parallel each other with participants from both ethnic groups (Teichman & Bar-Tal, 2008).

Recent data also suggest that differences in the relationship between national identification and in-group/out-group attitudes may be affected by gender and age (Oppenheimer, in press; Witvliet, 2004).

With this study we aim to obtain insights into the development of and relationship between strength of national identity and in-group/out-group attitudes with Bosnian-Bosniak and Bosnian-Serbian children and young adolescents.

METHOD

Participants

Eighty-nine Bosnian children aged 7 and 11 years participated in this study. They were divided over two ethnic groups consisting of 49 Bosnian-Bosniak and 40 Bosnian-Serbian children. Each ethnic groups consisted again of two age groups with mean ages 7.58 ($SD = 0.51$; $n = 23$) and 10.67 ($SD = 0.49$; $n = 18$) for the Bosnian-Bosniak participants and 7.33 ($SD = 0.58$; $n = 26$) and 10.71 ($SD = 0.48$; $n = 22$) for the Bosnian-Serbian participants. In each ethnic and age group approximately equal numbers of girls and boys were present. Parental permission as well as official permission of the Bosniak Ministry of Education and Science was obtained for the children's participation in this study.

Materials

The measures and procedure described by Barrett and Oppenheimer (2011, this issue) were used in this study. To ensure comprehensibility and compatibility, different translators first translated the The Strength of Identification Scale (SoIS) and the instructions from English to Bosnian and back again into English (Midzic, 2007). With the Bosnian-Bosniak children the × was substituted by *Bosnian* and with the Bosnian-Serbian children by *Serbian* resulting respectively in the following response possibilities to the question "Which one of these do you think best describes you?" (i.e., *degree* of national identification): "*very Bosnian [Serbian]*", "*quite Bosnian [Serbian]*", "*a little bit Bosnian [Serbian]*", and "*not at all Bosnian [Serbian]*".

With respect to the trait attribution task and affect questions, Bosnia, Serbia, and Croatia represented the in-group, traditional enemy out-group and neutral out-group depending on the child's national or ethnic background. Following the sorting task, the participants were asked to indicate on a 5-point Likert scale the extent to which they liked the in-group and the two out-groups.

Procedure

A team of two interviewers presented the measures to the children in the Bosnian language. One of the interviewers was a local university student.

The measures were individually presented to each child separately in a quiet room made available in their school. It was made clear to the children that the tasks did not represent tests and that there were no good or bad answers. In addition, they were informed that their responses would be treated completely anonymously. The participants were asked to report their age, gender, and ethnicity; this information was recorded on the individual answer sheets.

Following these explanations, the evaluation and the national identification task were presented in the latter but also the reversed order. No effect of order of presentation was observed. For full details of all three tasks and the randomization procedures that were employed in their administration, see Barrett and Oppenheimer (2011 this issue).

RESULTS

According to Barrett (2007), the six aspects of national identification should form a one-factor structure. An exploratory principal component analysis with varimax rotation resulted in a two-factor model with the Bosnian-Bosniak participants (*Determinant* = .355; *KMO* = .528; $\chi^2 = 44.70$, $df = 15$, $p < .001$). Both factors explained 59.6% of variance and showed importance, degree, pride, and affect to load on the first and positive and negative internalization on the second factor.

With the Bosnian-Serbian participants a three-factor model was present explaining 74.4% of the variance (*Determinant* = .250; *KMO* = .553; $\chi^2 = 46.01$, $df = 15$, $p < .001$). Here affect and pride loaded on the first, negative and positive internalization on the second, and importance and degree of national identification on the third factor. When a one-factor model for the data of the Bosniak and Serbian children was requested, two completely different structural models for national identification emerged (see Figures 1A and 1B).

Based on these findings, it appeared more sensible to perceive the aspects of national identification as separate variables and to examine the interrelations among in-group/out-group attitudes and the aspects of national identification separately for each ethnic group (in Table 1, the mean scores and standard deviations for the six aspects of national identification for each national group, age group and gender are presented). Consequently, first the analyses of the National Identity Scale are presented for the Bosnian-Bosniak and Bosnian-Serbian participants separately followed by comparative analyses.

National Identity Scale

Bosnian-Bosniak participants. A 2 × 2 (Age × Gender) multivariate analysis of variance (MANOVA) on the scores for the six SoIS dimensions of the Bosniak children did not reveal any significant interaction effects. A significant main effect for Age was present for degree, $F(1, 43) = 7.49$, $p < .01$, and importance of national identity, $F(1, 43) = 4.80$, $p < .05$, showing that with Bosniak children both the degree as well as the importance of national identification diminished across age (i.e., degree: 4.81 vs. 4.26 and importance: 4.81 vs. 4.18 for the 7- and 11-year-olds, respectively). For Gender only one significant main effect was present for the degree of national identification, $F(1, 43) = 6.59$, $p < .05$, showing girls to identify to a higher extent than boys with the Bosnian nation (i.e., 4.77 vs. 4.23).

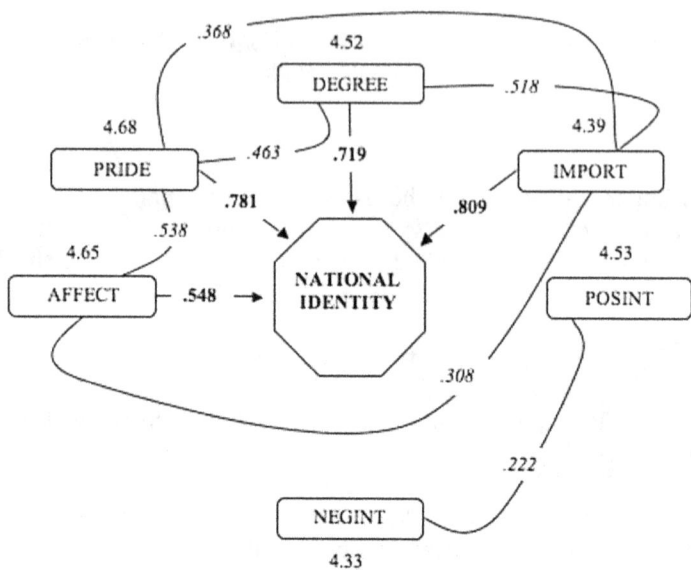

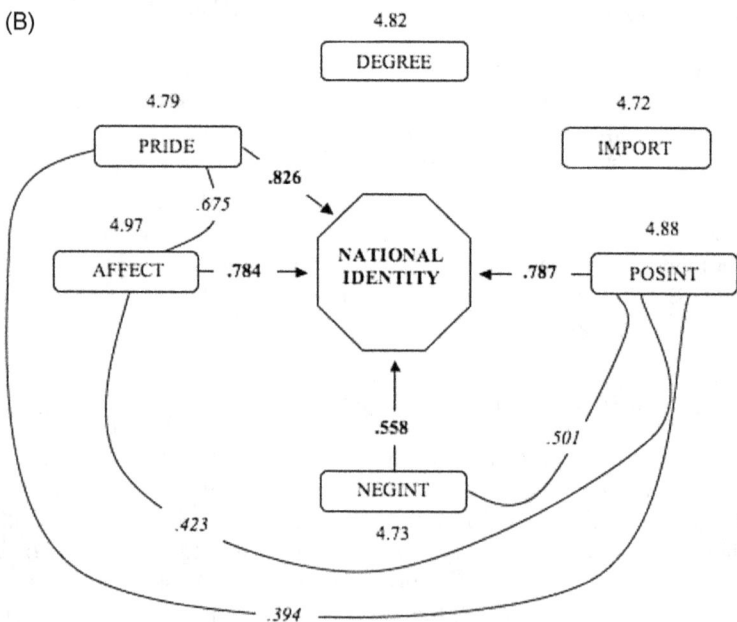

Figure 1. A schematic representation of the one-factor structure of national identification, showing the factor loadings for (**bold**), the mean scores of, and the correlations (*italics*) among the dimensions of national identification for the Bosnian-Bosniak (A) and Bosnian-Serbian children (B).

TABLE 1

Mean scores (and standard deviations) for the six aspects of national identification for the two national groups, age groups, and gender

| | Bosnian-Bosniak children | | | | | | | Bosnian-Serbian children | | | | | | |
| | 7 | | | 11 | | | All | 7 | | | 11 | | | All |
NI-aspects	Boy	Girl	Total	Boy	Girl	Total	Total	Boy	Girl	Total	Boy	Girl	Total	Total
Degree	4.63 (0.85)	5.00 (0.00)	4.81 (0.63)	3.87 (0.95)	4.60 (0.66)	4.26 (0.87)	4.51 (0.81)	5.00 (0.00)	4.53 (0.72)	4.83 (0.48)	4.78 (0.53)	4.83 (0.49)	4.80 (0.50)	4.81 (0.49)
Affect	4.82 (0.40)	4.50 (0.71)	4.67 (0.58)	4.58 (0.67)	4.64 (0.63)	4.62 (0.64)	4.64 (0.61)	5.00 (0.00)	4.83 (0.41)	4.94 (0.25)	5.00 (0.00)	5.00 (0.00)	5.00 (0.00)	4.97 (0.16)
PosInt	4.36 (1.21)	4.40 (0.52)	4.38 (0.92)	4.75 (0.45)	4.50 (0.52)	4.62 (0.50)	4.51 (0.72)	4.60 (0.52)	4.83 (0.41)	4.69 (0.48)	5.00 (0.00)	5.00 (0.00)	5.00 (0.00)	4.86 (0.35)
NegInt	4.27 (1.01)	4.60 (0.52)	4.43 (0.81)	4.25 (0.87)	4.21 (0.43)	4.23 (0.65)	4.32 (0.73)	4.50 (0.71)	4.50 (0.55)	4.50 (0.63)	4.85 (0.55)	5.00 (0.00)	4.90 (0.44)	4.73 (0.56)
Importance	5.00 (0.00)	4.60 (0.89)	4.81 (0.63)	4.02 (1.49)	4.31 (0.88)	4.18 (1.19)	4.46 (1.02)	4.72 (0.59)	5.00 (0.00)	4.83 (0.48)	4.78 (0.53)	4.35 (1.20)	4.62 (0.85)	4.71 (0.71)
Pride	4.87 (0.42)	4.72 (0.59)	4.80 (0.50)	4.55 (0.87)	4.60 (0.66)	4.58 (0.74)	4.68 (0.65)	4.86 (0.44)	4.57 (1.06)	4.75 (0.72)	4.89 (0.39)	4.83 (0.49)	4.87 (0.42)	4.82 (0.56)

Note: PosInt = Positive Internalization; NegInt = Negative Internalization.

Bosnian-Serbian participants.   The Age × Gender MANOVA with the Serbian children did not reveal any significant interaction effects nor a main effect for Gender. Two main effects for Age were present concerning positive internalization, $F(1, 33) = 6.70$, $p = .01$, and negative internalization, $F(1, 33) = 5.20$, $p < .05$. These findings show that when others evaluate their national identity positively and negatively, Serbian children at age 11 experience respectively more positive (i.e., 5.00 vs. 4.69) and more negative feelings (i.e., 4.91 vs. 4.50) than at age 7.

Bosnian-Bosniak versus Bosnian-Serbian participants.   A 2 × 2 × 2 (National Group × Age × Gender) MANOVA did not reveal a significant three-way interaction. While no significant effect for the Age by Gender interaction was evident (see also above), the National Group by Gender interaction was significant for the degree of identification only, $F(1, 76) = 7.13$, $p < .01$, indicating that Bosniak boys evidenced a significantly lower degree of national identification than Serbian boys (i.e., 4.23 vs. 4.88), while Bosniak girls showed a higher national identification than Serbian girls (i.e., 4.80 vs. 4.68). For the National Group by Age interaction two significant effects were present for degree of national identification, $F(1, 76) = 4.77$, $p < .05$, and negative internalization, $F(1, 76) = 4.47$, $p < .05$. With the Bosniak children the older children showed a significantly lower degree of identification than the younger children (i.e., 4.81 vs. 4.26), while the 7- and 11-year-old Serbian children did not differ in their degree of identification. With respect to negative internalization the Bosniak children demonstrated a decrease in negative feelings across age (i.e., 4.43 vs. 4.23) while the Serbian children showed an increase (i.e., 4.50 vs. 4.90).

The final analyses concerned the main effects of National Group, Age, and Gender. Whereas the Age and Gender effects are primarily important within each National Group (see above), the present analyses centred on the main effect for National Group. National Group was found to be significant for affect towards national identification, $F(1, 76) = 9.07$, $p < .01$, negative internalization, $F(1, 76) = 6.47$, $p < .05$, and positive internalization, $F(1, 76) = 7.23$, $p < .01$. These findings show that with respect to affect Serbian children attached higher positive affect to their national identification than Bosniak children (i.e., 4.97 vs. 4.64). With regard to negative internalization, Serbian children were more disturbed by negative evaluations about the Serbian nation than Bosniak children about the Bosnian nation (i.e., 4.73 vs. 4.32). Similarly, Serbian children appreciated positive evaluations about the Serbian nation more than Bosniak children about the Bosnian nation (i.e., 4.86 vs. 4.51).

In-group/out-group attitudes and affect

In the next section the data from the in-group/out-group attitudes are also presented for each national group separately followed by comparative analyses.

Bosnian-Bosniak participants. Analyses were conducted on the mean numbers of positive and negative traits assigned to the in-group (Bosnia), the traditional enemy out-group (Serbia), and a neutral out-group (Croatia) as well as on the difference scores based on the deduction of the negative from the positive traits for each group (see Table 2).

A 2 × 2 (Age × Gender) MANOVA on the positive and negative traits assigned to the groups revealed one significant interaction effect for positive traits for the neutral out-group, $F(1, 45) = 9.25, p < .01$, showing that Bosniak boys at age 7 evaluated the neutral out-group (i.e., Croatia) significantly less positively than at age 11 (i.e., 1.67 vs. 3.58), while girls showed the opposite trend (i.e., 4.27 vs. 2.50). For Gender one significant effect was evident with respect to negative evaluations of the neutral out-group, $F(1, 45) = 5.22$, $p < .05$, showing that Bosniak girls evaluated the Croatian nation less negatively than boys (i.e., 0.68 vs. 1.67). Finally, for Age also one significant effect was present dealing with negative evaluations of the in-group (i.e., Bosnia), $F(1, 45) = 4.00, p = .01$. This finding suggests that older children at age 11 evaluate the in-group more negatively than younger children at age 7 (i.e., 0.22 vs. 0.73).

When the negative evaluations for each group are deducted from the positive evaluations (i.e., the Pos.–Neg. scores; see Table 2), separate paired t-tests revealed that the in-group was evaluated significantly more positively than both out-groups, $t(48) = 8.62, p < .001$, and $t(48) = 5.46, p < .001$, for the Serbian and Croatian out-groups, respectively, while the Serbian out-group was also evaluated less positively than the neutral out-group (Croatia), $t(48) = 4.37, p < .001$.

Similarly, the traditional enemy out-group (Serbia) was evaluated significantly more negatively than the neutral out-group (Croatia), $t(48) = -5.55$, $p < .001$, and the in-group (Serbia), $t(48) = -6.80, p < .001$, while the neutral out-group was also evaluated more negatively than the in-group, $t(48) = -2.63, p < .05$.

With respect to the level of affect (i.e., liking) of the in-group and out-groups, a 2 × 2 MANOVA revealed a significant Age by Gender interaction for the level of likeability of the neutral out-group (i.e., Croatia), $F(1, 44) = 4.84, p < .05$, showing that whereas the older Bosniak boys (at age 11) liked the Croatians better than the younger boys (at age 7; 3.83 vs. 3.00), the older Bosniak girls liked the Croatians less than the younger girls (i.e., 4.27 vs. 4.08). In addition, girls liked the Croatian nation significantly better than boys (i.e., 4.17 vs. 3.42), $F(1, 44) = 10.51, p < .01$. No effect for Age was evident.

Bosnian-Serbian participants. With the Bosniak-Serbian children, an identical 2 × 2 (Age × Gender) MANOVA on the positive and negative traits assigned to the groups did not reveal any significant effect for the Age by Gender interaction nor for the main effect of Gender. Only one significant effect for Age was observed for positive evaluations of the

TABLE 2

The mean number of positive and negative trait attributions to and likeability ratings of the in-group and two out-groups by Bosnian-Bosniak and Bosnian-Serbian children

| | Bosnian-Bosniak children | | | |
| | Traits | | | |
	Pos.	Neg.	Pos.–Neg.	Liking
Bosnian-Bosniak children				
In-group: Bosnia	4.65	0.49	+4.16	4.92
Enemy out-group: Serbia	1.73	2.59	−0.86	3.00
Neutral out-group: Croatia	2.96	1.16	+1.80	3.79
Bosnian-Bosniak children				
In-group: Serbia	4.15	0.68	+3.48	4.85
Enemy out-group: Bosnia	1.40	2.80	−1.40	2.56
Neutral out-group: Croatia	2.25	1.77	+0.48	3.33

Note: Pos.–Neg. = deduction of negative from positive traits.

in-group, $F(1, 36) = 9.18$, $p < .01$, showing that at age 11 the in-group is significantly more positively evaluated than at age 7 (i.e., 4.73 vs. 3.44).

Paired t-tests comparing the positive and negative evaluations of the in-group, the traditional enemy out-group (i.e., Bosnia), and the neutral out-group (i.e., Croatia) revealed an identical pattern as was observed with the Bosnian-Bosniak children. Here, also, the traditional enemy out-group was evaluated less positively and more negatively than the in-group, $t(36) = 7.14$, $p < .001$, and $t(36) = -6.23$, $p < .001$, respectively, and the neutral out-group, $t(36) = -2.83$, $p < .01$, and $t(36) = -3.36$, $p < .01$, respectively.

A 2×2 (Age × Gender) MANOVA on the likeability scores with the Bosnian-Serbian children revealed only a significant effect for Age on the likeability scores for the in-group, $F(1, 35) = 4.09$, $p = .05$, showing that the older Serbian children liked Serbia more than the younger children (i.e., 5.00 vs. 4.67).

Bosnian-Bosniak versus Bosnian-Serbian participants. Comparisons by one-way ANOVA and paired t-test did not reveal any difference between both national groups in the extent of positive and negative evaluations of the own in-group, the traditional enemy out-groups, and the neutral out-group.

A $2 \times 2 \times 2$ (National Group × Age × Gender) MANOVA on the difference scores (i.e., calculated by deducting the negative from the positive ratings; see Table 2) revealed a significant effect for the three-way interaction of absolute evaluations of the neutral out-group (i.e., Croatia), $F(1, 81) = 6.27$, $p < .05$, showing that the Croatian nation is evaluated more positively by the Bosnian-Bosniak than the Bosnian-Serbian children, that boys evaluated the Croatian nation less positively than girls, and whereas no difference in the evaluations were present between the 7- and 11-year-old Bosniak children, the younger Serbian children evaluated the Croatians less positively than the older Serbian children. A significant Nation by Age interaction effect was present for the absolute evaluations of the in-group, $F(1, 81) = 6.19$, $p < .05$, showing that while older Bosniak children evaluated the in-group less positively than the younger Bosniak children (i.e., 3.61 vs. 4.78), the older Serbian children evaluated the in-group more positively than the younger Serbian children (i.e., 4.00 vs. 2.83).

With respect to the likeability ratings, an identical pattern of findings was observed suggesting that the absolute ratings of the in- and out-groups coincide with the likeability ratings. The correlation coefficients among these variables were all significant ($p < .001$) and ranged from .56 to .61.

National identification and in-group/out-group attitudes

The final part of the analyses involved the examination of relationships between dimensions of national identification and in-group/out-group attitudes. Based on the foregoing analyses correlation coefficients were calculated between the six dimensions of national identification and the three difference scores for in-group/out-group attitudes. Out of a total of 36 Pearson product–moment correlation coefficients, only two were found to be significant indicating the absence of any relationship between national identification and in-group/out-group attitudes. To check whether the small number of significant correlation coefficients is due to a non-normal distribution of the data, Spearman and Kendall's tau-b correlation coefficients were also calculated. The findings showed a reduction of the number of significant correlation coefficients from two to one.

DISCUSSION

The purpose of this study was to examine national identification, in-group/out-group attitudes, and the relationships among these variables with Bosnian-Bosniak and Bosnian-Serbian children aged 7 and 11.

Contrary to earlier findings with children across a range of ethnic and national groups (Barrett, 2007; see Barrett & Oppenheimer, this volume), the six dimensions of national identification did not form a unitary construct with either national group but related in different constellations to national identification for both groups. With the Bosniak children, the dimensions of importance, pride, degree, and affect contributed to national identification, while positive and negative internalization were not part of the construct. With the Bosnian-Serbian children, positive and negative internalization, pride, and affect constituted the contributing dimensions of national identification, while degree and importance did not play any role. It appears that the Bosnian-Serbian children, as a minority in Bosnia, were considerably more sensitive to positive and negative comments about their own nation than the Bosniak children.

The absence of a unitary construct of national identification demanded the separate examination of each dimension. Most interesting was the finding that overall the Serbian children attached more importance to their national identification than Bosniak children. They showed a considerably higher degree of identification as well as attached more importance to national identification than the Bosniak children. Nevertheless, the higher degree and greater importance of national identification with Serbian children were not related to their higher sensitivity to positive and negative comments about their own nation. That is, the reaction to outside evaluations did not affect the degree and importance of national identification.

Causes of this higher national identification with the Serbian children may be found in the hallways of Serbian schools that were filled with drawings of old national heroes and saints through which children were made aware of their ethnic belonging on an every-day basis. Also, the experience of the Serbian population in Bosnia of being the black sheep may have reinforced their feelings of pride and importance of their national identification. Nevertheless, it is important to mention that the Bosniak and Serbian groups both scored high on the scales, implying that one's belonging to an ethnic group plays an important role in Bosnia-Herzegovina. That is, many of the children had maximum scores on the identification questions. These high scores and the breakdown of the theoretically assumed unitary structure of national identification may have resulted in the absence of significant associations between national identification and in-group/out-group attitudes.

Bosnian-Bosniak as well as the Bosnian-Serbian children rated their own in-group more positively and less negatively than the "neutral" out-group (i.e., Croatia) and the traditional enemy out-group (i.e., Serbia for the Bosniak children and Bosnia for the Serbian children). In addition, Bosniak and Serbian children rated each other the least positive and the most negative, with the Croatian out-group being in second place among both groups. This could be explained by the fact that during the war the Croatian army fought initially together with Bosniak forces against Serbia. Half-way through the war, Croatian forces switched sides and continued fighting together with Serbian forces against Bosniak forces while during the whole war, Bosniak and Serbian forces fought against each other.

Because the present study served as a pilot study for the other studies reported in this volume, no additional "real" neutral country was included in the study. Consequently, it is difficult to examine the extent to which Croatia was considered as a real neutral out-group or partly as a neutral out-group and partly as an additional enemy out-group.

According to Aboud and Amato (2001; Aboud, 1988), a developmental change in the development of racial and ethnic prejudice takes place between the ages of 6 and 11. At the age of 6, children should show high positive attitudes toward their own ethnic in-group and high negative attitudes towards ethnic out-groups. From the age of 6, a reduction in in-group favouritism and racial prejudice toward ethnic out-groups should occur, resulting in a more balanced view of the in-group and out-groups around the age of 11 years.

In the present study, only partial support for Aboud's conclusion was present. Whereas the 11-year-old Bosniak children evaluated their in-group (i.e., Bosnia) less positively than the 7-year-old Bosniak children, the older Serbian children evaluated their in-group (i.e., Serbia) more positively than younger Serbian children. A possible explanation for this finding may be the fact that national identity of young Serbian children (age of 7) is not yet strongly present and that they identify with their own group as well as the "enemy" group, because the Serbs were defeated by the Bosnians. At this point Teichman's and Bar-Tal's (2008) assumption that in the context of an intractable conflict, an increased in-group preference and out-group derogation should be evident with pre- and early adolescents is valid for the Bosniak participants (i.e., the majority), but not the Serbian participants (i.e., the minority). That is, Serbian children living in Bosnia may feel under much greater threat than the Bosniak children. This threat may affect national identification processes in particular at younger ages. Because children from the age of 7 to 11 start to categorize themselves as members of their own national group (i.e., Serbia; Aboud & Amato, 2001) more positive attitudes towards the in-group to which they belong may develop. Bosniak children have a clear preference for their own ethnic group. While Bosnian-Bosniak as well as Bosnian-Serbian children show relatively high levels of nationalism at age 11, in particular during adolescence, Serbian children are more nationalistic than Bosniak children (Midzic, 2007).

The assumption that a higher degree of national identification would result in more positive attitudes toward the in-group and the more negative attitudes toward the out-groups could not be confirmed by the age groups involved in the present study. No direct relationships were evident between the dimensions of national identification and in-group/out-group attitudes. As was noted above, this finding may be due to the absence of a coherent structure of national identification at the studied ages. Within this context, it is important to note that Midzic (2007) observed the presence of such relationships with Bosniak and Serbian adolescents. Apparently, in post-conflict Bosnia-Herzegovina, the awareness and meaning of national identification develop gradually and become more evident from the age of 11, resulting in differences in level of "nationalism" between the two ethnic groups as well as clear contributions of dimensions of national identification to in-group/out-group attitudes in adolescence.

Besides the absence of a "real" neutral out-group, a second limitation of the present study should be mentioned. Unfortunately, it was not possible to find one principal of a Croatian school in Sarajevo willing to participate in the study. Because school policy of the Croatian schools was directed towards equality of all nations, the theme of the present study was thought too delicate and to contradict the goals of this policy. Nevertheless, it would have been very interesting to see how Croatian children rate their own in-group and in particular the two out-groups.

What becomes clear is that, almost 14 years after the war, a lot of work still needs to be done before reconciliation will be achieved between the different ethnic or national groups in Bosnia-Herzegovina. If a united country is to evolve, special attention has to be paid to the welfare of children of minority groups and to the cultivation of empathetic attitudes towards the other ethnic groups (Garrod et al., 2003). Schools and the educational system may play an important role in this task. As Dr Adil Pasalic-Kreso, presently member of the Senate of the University of Sarajevo, noted in a public speech:

> Everyone involved in education, including every teacher, must recognize his/her duty, always staying aware of issues triggering prejudices and negative affect towards other ethnical groups. ... Such an approach will encourage the development of liberal, creative, and multicultural students. Without this determination to create an inclusive educational environment for all, current and future pledges to democracy and multiculturalism will remain superficial. (see also Pasalic-Kreso, 1999)

Most importantly, however, the present study offers support for Barrett's (2007) assumption that the strength of national identification and inter-group attitudes varies considerably as a function of children's "own psychological characteristics, the groups to which they belong, and the particular societal contexts in which they live" (Barrett & Oppenheimer, 2011 this issue, p. 14).

REFERENCES

Aboud, F. E. (1988). *Children and prejudice.* Oxford, UK: Blackwell.

Aboud, F. E., & Amato, M. (2001). Developmental and socialization influences on intergroup bias. In R. Brown & S. L. Gaertner (Eds.), *Blackwell handbook of social psychology: Intergroup processes* (pp. 65–85). Oxford, UK: Blackwell.

Augoustinos, M., & Rosewarne, D. L. (2001). Stereotype knowledge and prejudice in children. *British Journal of Developmental Psychology, 19,* 143–156.

Bar-On, D. (2006). Stereotypes and prejudice in conflict: Representations of Arabs in Israeli-Jewish society [Review]. *Israel Studies, 11*(2), 75–80.

Barrett, M. (1996). English children's acquisition of a European identity. In G. Breakwell & E. Lyons (Eds.), *Changing European identities: Social psychological analyses of social change* (pp. 349–369). Oxford, UK: Butterworth-Heinemann.

Barrett, M. (2007). *Children's knowledge, beliefs and feelings about nations and national groups.* Hove, UK: Psychology Press.

Barrett, M., & Oppenheimer, L. (2011). Findings, theories and methods in the study of children's national identifications and national attitudes. *European Journal of Developmental Psychology, 8,* 5–24.

Barrett, M., Wilson, H., & Lyons, E. (2003). The development of national ingroup bias: English children's attributions of characteristics to English, American and German people. *British Journal of Developmental Psychology, 21,* 193–220.

Bar-Tal, D. (1996). Development of social categories and stereotypes in early childhood: The case of "the Arab" concept formation, stereotype and attitudes by Jewish children in Israel. *International Journal of Intercultural Relations, 20,* 341–370.

Bar-Tal, D. (2010). Culture of conflict: Evolvement, institutionalization, and consequences. In R. Schwarzer & P. A. French (Eds.), *Personality, human development, and culture: International perspectives on psychological science* (Vol. 2, pp. 183–198). Hove, UK: Psychology Press.

Bennett, M., Lyons, E., Sani, F., & Barrett, M. (1998). Children's subjective identification with the group and ingroup favoritism. *Developmental Psychology, 34,* 902–909.

Garrod, A., Beal, C. R., Thomas, J., Jaeger, W., Davis, J., Hodzic, A., et al. (2003). Culture, ethnic conflict and moral orientation in Bosnian children. *Journal of Moral Education, 32,* 131–150.

Midzic, E. (2007). *National identity and ingroup–outgroup attitudes as determinants of enemy images and the understanding of the concept of enemy in Dutch and Bosnian children.* Unpublished MA thesis, University of Amsterdam, NL.

Oppenheimer, L. (in press). National identification of Dutch youth: An exploratory study. *Journal of Adolescence.*

Pasalic-Kreso, A. (1999). Education in Bosnia and Herzegovina: Minority inclusion and majority rules. *Current Issues in Comparative Education, 2,* 6–13.

Povrzanovic, M. (1997). Children, war and nation: Croatia 1991–4. *Childhood: A Global Journal of Child Research, 4,* 81–102.

Rutland, A. (1999). The development of national prejudice, ingroup favoritism and self-stereotypes in British children. *British Journal of Social Psychology, 38,* 55–70.

Teichman, Y., & Bar-Tal, D. (2008). Acquisition and development of a shared psychological intergroup repertoire in a context of intractable conflict. In S. M. Quintana & C. McKown (Eds.), *Handbook of race, racism, and the developing child* (pp. 452–482). Hoboken, NJ: Wiley.

Witvliet, M. (2004). *Attitudes about in- and outgroups and the enemy image of children.* Unpublished MA thesis, University of Amsterdam. Amsterdam, NL.

EUROPEAN JOURNAL OF DEVELOPMENTAL PSYCHOLOGY
2011, 8 (1), 58–73

Ψ Psychology Press
Taylor & Francis Group

National identity and in-group/out-group attitudes: Catholic and Protestant children in Northern Ireland

Elizabeth Gallagher and Ed Cairns

Department of Psychology, University of Ulster, Coleraine, Northern Ireland

This study investigated national identity and intergroup attitudes and how strength of national identity impacts on in-group and out-group attitudes. The data were gathered in post-violence Northern Ireland with children aged 7 and 11 years of age. A total of 148 children took part (Catholic participants: $n = 73$ and Protestant participants: $n = 75$). Eight schools were selected, 4 Protestant schools and 4 Catholic schools. Children were individually interviewed in the school setting. A significant positive correlation between strength of national identity and affect towards the in-group was found for Protestant participants. A significant negative correlation between strength of national identity and affect towards the traditional enemy was found for Catholic participants. There was also evidence of in-group bias, in that both Protestant and Catholic children evaluated their own group more positively than the other out-groups. In addition, it was found that younger children are more sensitive to negative comments about their own national identity than older children. These findings are discussed in terms of previous findings and theoretical perspectives.

Keywords: National identity; Intergroup conflict; Northern Ireland.

INTRODUCTION

Northern Ireland has a long history of conflict based on a struggle between those who wish to see it remain part of the UK (mainly Protestants) and those who wish (mainly Catholics) to have a united Ireland (Cairns & Darby, 1998). It has been described as being a historical, religious, political, economical and psychological conflict (Whyte, 1990). People in Northern Ireland have endured 30 years of conflict. As a consequence of the violence

Correspondence should be addressed to Ed Cairns, Department of Psychology, University of Ulster, Coleraine, Northern Ireland, BT52 1SA, UK. E-mail: e.cairns@ulster.ac.uk

DOI: 10.1080/17405629.2010.533977

3,600 people have died and approximately 40,000 have been injured. Although Northern Ireland is now in a post-conflict phase, it still remains deeply divided and trust between communities remains fragile (Hewstone et al., 2005). For example, housing and education have become more segregated and do not show any signs of improving, especially in working-class areas (Hughes, 2003). The majority of people still live in single identity communities either Protestant or Catholic and 97% of Northern Irish population attend religion-specific schools (Church, Visser, & Johnson, 2004; Gallagher, 1995). It has been argued that, although segregation is a result of the conflict and not the cause, it lends a hand in maintaining prejudice and religious stereotyping (e.g., Gallagher, 1995; Hewstone et al., 2005; Tausch, Hewstone, Kenworthy, Cairns, & Christ, 2007).

In light of this, it is not surprising that national identity is at the heart of the conflict in Northern Ireland (Trew, 1986; Waddell & Cairns, 1991). People view their alliance to one or the other conflicting religious-based communities as the most important aspect of their identity within their country (Cairns & Mercer, 1984). According to Devine and Schubotz (2004), from their survey in 2003 of 16-year-olds in Northern Ireland the majority of participants (60%) said that their national identity was important to them in comparison to 15% who said that national identity was not important to them.

The impact of political violence on children in Northern Ireland has been extensively studied (see Cairns, 1987, 2001; Cairns & Cairns, 1995; Cairns, Wilson, Gallagher, & Trew, 1995; Connolly & Maginn, 1999; Gough, Robinson, Kremer, & Mitchell, 1992; Trew, 1992, for detailed summaries). Nevertheless, only limited research has examined young children's strength of national identity and how this impacts on intergroup attitudes. Despite the fact that there is evidence to suggest that sectarian attitudes are formed at an early age. For example, according to recent research that by the age of six, 90% of children are aware of the community divide in Northern Ireland, a third identify with one part of the community and 15% are making sectarian comments (Connolly, Smith, & Kelly, 2002).

According to social identity theory (SIT; Tajfel & Turner, 1979), there is a direct association between identification with a social group and tendencies towards bias, discrimination and intergroup conflict. SIT was originally developed by Tajfel (1978; Tajfel & Turner, 1979, 1986) and has been used to explain why people discriminate against out-groups and favour their own group. Social identity is defined as "that part of an individual's self-concept which derives from his [or her] knowledge of his [or her] membership of a social group (or groups) together with the value and emotional significance attached to that membership" (Tajfel, 1978, p. 63). The occurrence of in-group bias is explained in terms of conflicting interests and subjective identification with one's own group. According to SIT when children come to categorize and identify themselves as part of their national group, they will show preference for that group and strive to differentiate themselves positively from other groups. Also, strength of national identification is predicted to affect the level of in-group bias (see Reizábal, Valencia, & Barrett, 2004, for empirical support).

Social identity development theory (SIDT), on the other hand, proposes that national and ethnic identities develop through a sequence of stages. One of the final stages is when children become increasingly identified with the in-group, they begin to adopt the negative attitudes already established within the in-group and thus, at around the age of 7 years old, children become focused upon out-groups through actively disliking them (Nesdale, 2004, 2008).

However, the development of children's intergroup attitudes can vary and be impacted by a number of factors. For instance, the theory developed by Teichman and Bar-Tal (2008), identified as an integrative developmental contextual theory (IDCT), takes into account the role of intractable conflicts in the development of children's stereotypes and prejudices (Teichman & Bar-Tal, 2008). IDCT proposes that multiple factors in a given social context simultaneously influence the shared psychological intergroup repertoire (SPIR), which consists of the critical elements of sociopsychological infrastructure that develops in the context of a conflict and these elements include conflicts over territory, resources, or values, and produce stereotypes, prejudices, associated emotions, and behavioural intentions towards the rival group (Teichman & Bar-Tal, 2008). According to IDCT all the factors involved in the development of SPIRs (affect, cognitive, and identity development) are active all along the developmental span. In different stages, a different factor has the potential for acquiring salience and major influence, but the salience of each factor may be influenced by past experiences or contextual conditions. IDCT suggests that at school age cognitive development may be the leading force guiding social biases and that during pre- and early adolescence identity development becomes the guiding force (Teichman & Bar-Tal, 2008).

An additional theory that takes into account all the different factors, which can impact on the development of children's intergroup attitudes, is societal-social-cognitive-motivational theory (SSCMT) devised by Barrett (2007). According to SSCMT all of the following are available as potential sources of information about national identity for the child—state, racial and ethnic groups; parental discourse and practices; the school curriculum and school textbooks; teachers discourse and practices; peer group discourse and practices; and the representational content of the mass media. SSCMT postulates that it is from all of these various sources that children can potentially acquire information about the pattern of relationships between their in-group and out-groups, and the relative status of their in-group within this broader structure of intergroup relations.

A particular concern in Northern Ireland has been with the impact that political violence and social divisions have had on children. Children in Northern Ireland may have experienced an indirect effect of the conflict through factors such as socialization, parents, etc. For example, the Young Life and Times Survey in Northern Ireland found that half of the respondents said that their families are central to their views of the other religious community (Devine & Schubotz, 2004). The present study assessed the development of national identity and the impact of strength of national identity on intergroup attitudes of children in post-conflict Northern Ireland

METHOD

Participants

A total of 148 participants took part in this study. A total of 73 Catholic participants (males $n = 34$, females $n = 39$) and 75 Protestant participants (males $n = 43$, females $n = 32$). The sample was obtained from eight primary schools in Northern Ireland (four Protestant schools and four Catholic schools). Each group consisted of two age groups with mean ages 7.51 ($SD = 0.76$; $n = 39$) and 11.40 ($SD = 0.33$; $n = 34$) for Catholic participants and 7.41 ($SD = 0.33$; $n = 37$) and 11.22 ($SD = 0.65$; $n = 38$) for Protestant participants. All children were of White ethnicity. Parental permission as well as ethical approval by the Ethical Review Committee of the School of Psychology and by the Ethical Review Board of the University of Ulster was obtained for the children's participation in this study.

Materials

National identification.   Children were asked five questions designed to assess their strength of national identification. These questions form the strength of identification scale (SoIS) designed by Barrett (2007) with Catholic children responding to the identity "Irish" and Protestant children to the identity "British".

In-group/out-group attitudes.   Attitudes of the children towards various national groups was assessed using two methods: a trait attribution task and a like–dislike affect measure. The trait attribution task elicited the children's descriptions of their in-group and three out-groups. For Catholic children the in-group was Irish people and the first out-group was British people, commonly perceived as the traditional enemy, the two other out-groups were Scottish people and German people, both considered to be relatively neutral out-groups. For Protestant children the in-group was British people and the first out-group was Irish people, commonly perceived to be the traditional enemy, and the two other out-groups were Scottish people and German people, both considered to be relatively neutral out-groups.

Immediately after the completion of each trait attribution task, the child was asked: "Now, I just want to ask you one more thing about × people. Do you like or dislike × people?" If the child indicated either liking or disliking they were asked: "How much? Do you like/dislike them a lot or a little?" For full details of all the tasks and the procedures that were employed in their administration, see Barrett and Oppenheimer (2011 this issue).

RESULTS

National Identification

According to previous research the six aspects of National Identification should form a one-factor structure (Barrett, 2007). An exploratory principal component analysis with varimax rotation resulted in a two-factor model with Catholic participants (*Determinant* = .387; *KMO* = .564; $\chi^2 = 56.23$, $df = 15.000$, $p < .001$). Both factors explained 35% of variance and showed importance, degree, pride, and affect to load on the first and positive and negative internalization on the second factor. With the Protestant participants a one-factor model was present explaining 53% of the variance (*Determinant* = .130; *KMO* = .834; $\chi^2 = 104.525$, $df = 15.000$, $p < .001$). Here, degree, affect, negative internalization, positive internalization, importance and pride all loaded on the factor. Based on these findings, it appeared more sensible to perceive the aspects of National Identification as separate variables and to examine the interrelations among in-group/out-group attitudes and the aspects of National Identification separately for each group (see Table 1).

National Identity Scale

Children's levels of National Identification and whether changes were observed as a function of age, gender and national group were analysed by a 2 × 2 × 2 (Age × Gender × National Group) multivariate analysis of variance (MANOVA). The National Identification Scale is made up of 6 variables: Degree of national identity, affect, positive internalization, negative internalization, importance, and pride. Separate analyses were conducted for each variable.

A significant difference was found for degree of national identity and national group, $F(1, 118) = 5.22$, $p < .01$, with Catholic participants

TABLE 1

Mean scores (and standard deviations) for the six aspects of National Identification for the two national groups, age groups, and gender

| NI-aspects | Catholic children | | | | | | | Protestant children | | | | | | |
| | 7 | | | 11 | | | All | 7 | | | 11 | | | All |
	Boy	Girl	Total	Boy	Girl	Total	Total	Boy	Girl	Total	Boy	Girl	Total	Total
Degree	3.67 (0.82)	3.17 (1.38)	3.39 (1.17)	3.36 (0.84)	3.31 (0.70)	3.33 (0.76)	3.37 (0.99)	3.29 (0.82)	2.73 (1.10)	3.04 (0.98)	3.21 (0.79)	2.64 (1.03)	3.00 (0.91)	3.02 (0.93)
Affect	4.73 (0.70)	4.67 (0.69)	4.70 (0.68)	4.50 (0.65)	4.69 (0.48)	4.60 (0.56)	4.65 (0.63)	4.64 (0.50)	4.36 (0.81)	4.52 (0.65)	4.21 (0.85)	4.18 (0.98)	4.20 (0.89)	4.35 (0.80)
PosInt	4.60 (0.51)	4.67 (0.48)	4.64 (0.49)	4.50 (0.65)	4.56 (0.63)	4.53 (0.63)	4.59 (0.56)	4.64 (0.50)	4.64 (0.50)	4.64 (0.49)	4.63 (0.50)	4.36 (0.67)	4.53 (0.57)	4.58 (0.53)
NegInt	4.67 (0.49)	4.83 (0.38)	4.76 (0.43)	4.21 (0.70)	4.06 (1.06)	4.13 (0.90)	4.46 (0.76)	4.86 (0.36)	4.45 (0.82)	4.68 (0.63)	4.37 (0.77)	4.18 (0.87)	4.30 (0.79)	4.47 (0.74)
Importance	3.53 (0.52)	3.17 (0.98)	3.33 (0.82)	3.29 (0.47)	3.37 (0.72)	3.33 (0.61)	3.33 (0.72)	3.36 (0.63)	2.73 (0.90)	3.08 (0.81)	2.79 (0.63)	2.91 (0.74)	2.83 (0.67)	2.95 (0.73)
Pride	3.60 (0.63)	3.56 (0.70)	3.58 (0.66)	3.36 (0.50)	3.62 (0.50)	3.50 (0.51)	3.54 (0.59)	3.43 (0.65)	2.91 (0.83)	3.20 (0.76)	3.05 (0.97)	2.82 (0.98)	2.97 (0.96)	3.07 (0.88)

Note: PosInt = Positive Internalization; NegInt = Negative Internalization.

($M = 3.37$, $SD = 0.99$) showing a higher degree of national identity in comparison to Protestant participants ($M = 3.02$, $SD = 0.93$). A significant main effect was also found for degree of national identity and Gender, $F(1, 118) = 5.44$, $p < .05$, with males ($M = 3.37$, $SD = 0.81$) showing a significantly higher degree of national identity than females ($M = 3.02$, $SD = 1.10$).

In terms of affect towards national identity and national group a significant difference was found, $F(1, 118) = 4.90$, $p < .05$, with Catholic participants ($M = 4.65$, $SD = 0.63$) showing greater affect towards national identity in comparison to Protestant participants ($M = 4.35$, $SD = 0.80$)

A significant difference was found for negative internalization and Age group, $F(1, 118) = 13.86$, $p < .05$, with 7-year-olds ($M = 4.72$, $SD = 0.52$) showing significantly higher negative internalization of national identity than 11-year-olds ($M = 4.22$, $SD = 0.85$).

No significant differences were found for positive internalization of national identity.

A significant difference was found for importance of national identity and national group, $F(1, 118) = 8.65$, $p < .01$, with Catholic participants ($M = 3.33$, $SD = 0.72$) having a higher level of importance of national identity in comparison to Protestant participants ($M = 2.95$, $SD = 0.73$).

In terms of pride towards own nationality and national group a significant main effect was found, $F(1, 118) = 12.15$, $p < .01$, with Catholic participants ($M = 3.54$, $SD = 0.59$) showing a greater level of pride towards their own nationality in comparison to Protestant participants ($M = 3.07$, $SD = 0.88$).

Attitudes towards the national in-group and out-groups

Attitudes towards each national group were analysed in terms of total number of positive adjectives and total number of negative adjectives using a $2 \times 2 \times 2$ (Age × Gender × National Group) MANOVA (see Tables 2 and 3).

Analysis of the relationship between Catholic participants' overall positivity scores for out-group 1 (British) with Gender showed significant effects, $F(1, 73) = 5.97$, $p < .05$, with males ($M = 1.32$, $SD = 1.20$) having a lower positivity towards out-group 1 (British) than females ($M = 2.08$, $SD = 1.34$).

Analysis of the relationship between Protestant positivity scores for out-group 2 (Scottish) and Age group showed significant effects, $F(1, 75) = 5.62$, $p < .05$, with 7-year-olds ($M = 1.76$, $SD = 1.23$) having a lower positivity in comparison to 11-year-olds ($M = 2.42$, $SD = 1.20$). Both groups attributed the highest amount of positive adjectives to the in-group.

Analysis of the relationship between Catholic participants' overall negativity scores for out-group 1 (British) and Gender showed significant

TABLE 2

Means (and standard deviations) for the total number of positive adjectives for each national group according to age, gender for Catholic and Protestant participants

Catholic children

	7			11		
	B	G	Total	B	G	Total
In-group: Irish	2.78 (0.43)	2.86 (0.57)	2.82 (0.51)	2.94 (0.44)	2.89 (0.58)	2.91 (0.51)
Enemy out-group: British	1.28 (1.37)	2.14 (1.28)	1.74 (1.37)	1.38 (1.02)	2.00 (1.45)	1.71 (1.29)
Neutral out-group: Scottish	1.67 (0.97)	2.24 (1.18)	1.97 (1.11)	2.38 (1.02)	2.33 (1.19)	2.35 (1.10)
Neutral out-group: German	1.56 (1.04)	2.00 (1.09)	1.79 (1.08)	2.06 (1.34)	2.33 (1.64)	2.21 (1.49)

Protestant children

	7			11		
	B	G	Total	B	G	Total
In-group: British	3.05 (1.15)	2.59 (1.00)	2.84 (1.09)	3.17 (0.89)	3.13 (1.19)	3.16 (1.00)
Enemy out-group: Irish	1.55 (1.54)	1.71 (0.98)	1.62 (1.30)	1.78 (1.41)	2.07 (0.96)	1.89 (1.25)
Neutral out-group: Scottish	1.40 (1.31)	2.18 (1.01)	1.76 (1.23)	2.30 (1.29)	2.60 (1.06)	2.42 (1.20)
Neutral out-group: German	1.20 (1.28)	1.18 (0.88)	1.19 (1.10)	1.74 (1.96)	1.53 (1.41)	1.66 (1.74)

TABLE 3

Means (and standard deviations) for the total number of negative adjectives for each national group according to age, gender for Catholic and Protestant participants

Catholic children

	7			11		
	B	G	Total	B	G	Total
In-group: Irish	0.00 (0.00)	0.00 (0.00)	0.00 (0.00)	0.06 (0.00)	0.06 (0.00)	0.06 (0.00)
Enemy out-group: British	1.83 (1.25)	0.62 (0.80)	1.18 (1.19)	1.19 (1.51)	0.56 (0.86)	0.85 (1.23)
Neutral out-group: Scottish	0.39 (0.98)	0.24 (0.44)	0.31 (0.73)	0.19 (0.54)	0.22 (0.55)	0.21 (0.54)
Neutral out-group: German	0.50 (0.71)	0.38 (0.67)	0.44 (0.68)	0.44 (0.63)	0.17 (0.38)	0.29 (0.52)

Protestant children

	7			11		
	B	G	Total	B	G	Total
In-group: British	0.20 (0.41)	0.29 (0.47)	0.24 (0.43)	0.17 (0.58)	0.47 (0.74)	0.29 (0.65)
Enemy out-group: Irish	1.45 (1.79)	0.88 (1.11)	1.19 (1.52)	1.26 (1.79)	0.53 (0.64)	0.97 (1.48)
Neutral outgroup: Scottish	0.95 (1.05)	0.35 (0.70)	0.68 (0.94)	0.52 (0.79)	0.33 (1.05)	0.45 (0.89)
Neutral outgroup: German	1.05 (1.10)	0.94 (1.09)	1.00 (1.08)	1.43 (1.44)	1.13 (1.25)	1.32 (1.36)

effects, $F(1, 73) = 12.31$, $p < .01$, with males ($M = 1.53$, $SD = 1.40$) showing a greater negativity than females ($M = 0.59$, $SD = 0.82$). No significant effects were found for Age.

Analysis of the relationship between Protestant participants' overall negativity scores for out-group 1 (Irish) and Age and Gender showed no significant effects.

The least amount of negative adjectives was attributed to the in-group. The highest amount of negative adjectives was attributed to out-group 1 (i.e., the traditional enemy).

National Identification and affect towards the national in-group and out-groups

The relationship between strength of National Identification and affect toward each national group and whether this changes or develops as a function of age, was explored. Using partial correlations the relationship was analysed for both groups while controlling for age.

This revealed strong, positive correlations between affect towards the in-group and affect towards the in-group ($r = .31$, $p < .05$) and negative internalization ($r = .45$, $p < .001$), importance ($r = .47$, $p < .001$), and pride of national identification ($r = .31$, $p < .05$) for Protestant participants. For Catholic participants no statistically significant correlations were present.

Negative correlations were found between affect towards out-group 1 (i.e., the traditional enemy) and the dimensions of affect towards out-group 1 (the traditional enemy) ($r = -.36$, $p < .01$) and pride of national identification ($r = -.38$, $p < .01$) for Catholic participants. For Protestant participants no statistically significant correlations were present. No significant correlations were found for the other out-groups.

National Identification and attitudes towards the national in-group and out-groups

The data was analysed to explore the relationship between strength of National Identification, the total number of positive attributes and negative attributes given to each national group. Partial correlations were used to examine the relationship, partialling out age.

There was a significant positive correlation between Protestant participants National Identifications and attitudes towards the in-group ($r = .41$, $p < .01$).

A significantly negative correlation was found for National Identification and attitudes towards out-group 1 (traditional enemy) for both Catholics ($r = .28$, $p < .05$) and Protestants ($r = .23$, $p < .05$).

DISCUSSION

The purpose of this study was to examine national identification, and in-group/out-group attitudes among 7- and 11-year-old Catholic and Protestant children in Northern Ireland. The present study partly supports the findings obtained by Barrett and Lyons (2001) with British children, in that the six dimensions of National Identification did form a unitary construct for Protestant children. However, for the Catholic children in the study the dimensions of degree, affect, importance and pride contributed to National Identification while both positive and negative internalization were not part of the construct. It appears that Protestant children, although a majority in Northern Ireland were considerably more sensitive to both positive and negative comments about their national group than the Catholic children in the study. The present study found that Catholic participants showed a higher degree of national identity, affect towards national identity, importance and greater pride of national identity in comparison to Protestant participants.

Previous studies have reported that most children, tend to display a positive sense of pride in, and to give positive ratings of, their own country and this positive sense of pride can be present in children at 7 years of age of (Amadeo, Torney-Purta, Lehmann, Husfeldt, & Nikolova, 2002; Hess & Torney, 1967; Jaspers, Van de Geer, Tajfel, & Johnson, 1972; Johnson, Middleton, & Tajfel, 1970). Boys also tend to exhibit higher levels of pride than females. However these differences can vary from country to country. The present study found that Catholic participants showed a more positive sense of pride in comparison to Protestant participants. The data also showed that 7-year-old children are more sensitive to negative comments made by others about their national identity and experience more negative feeling than the 11-year-olds in the study. Moreover, while some children rate their own country as being better than all other countries (Hess & Torney, 1967; Nugent, 1994), other children may rate other countries as being just as good as, if not better than, their own country (Dennis, Lindberg, & McCrone, 1972; Middleton, Tajfel, & Johnson, 1970).

The present study found that both groups showed in-group favouritism by attributing the highest amount of positive adjectives and the least amount of negative adjectives to the in-group. The study also assessed whether groups that are the traditional enemies of the child's own in-group would be evaluated less positively than out-groups by the children. The present study found that Catholic children evaluated the traditional enemy (British) less positively than all other out-groups. Gender differences were also found in that Catholic boys evaluated the traditional enemy (British) less positively than Catholic females. However, Protestant children did not rate the traditional enemy (Irish) less positively than the other out-groups, in fact they evaluated a neutral out-group (Germans) less positively than the other out-groups. In terms of evaluating the in-group and out-groups negatively the present study found that both groups had evaluated the in-group less negatively than the other out-groups. Catholic children attributed the least amount of negative adjectives to the in-group with 7-year-old children attributing no negative adjectives to the in-group.

Children develop a range of different attitudes towards other groups depending on the country or society that they grow up in. However, their own national group is often favoured more positively than other groups and groups within their country that are perceived to be the traditional enemy whether a historical or current enemy are evaluated less positively (Barrett, 2007; Jahoda, 1962). According to social identity development theory (SIDT) in countries that feel under threat from other countries and where negative attitudes towards the "enemy" are common the occurrence of negative attitudes towards "enemy" nations may appear after the age of 7 in children in these situations (Nesdale, 2004, 2008).

According to integrative developmental contextual theory (IDCT) in the context of intractable conflict, as a consequence of perceived threat from the target out-group, prejudice and social biases do not moderate with age (Teichman & Bar-Tal, 2008). In divided societies such as Northern Ireland contextual influences lead to an increased awareness of threat, salience of group differences, and the intensity of national identity, and the cognitive development occurring at the age of 7 to 9 years does not reduce in-group positivity and out-group negativity. The patterns manifested by younger children transcends into pre- and early adolescence in which in-group preference and out-group derogation is amplified (Teichman & Bar-Tal, 2008). In such divided communities as Northern Ireland, an important aspect of the development of national identity under such segregated circumstances may result in a conflictual relationship with the "perceived traditional enemy" out-group (Livingstone & Haslam, 2008).

The present study also attempted to assess how strength of national identity impacts on children's affect towards their own group and other out-groups and also their attitudes toward different groups. The present study found that for Protestant participants, strength of national identity was positively correlated with affect towards the in-group and positive attitudes. Therefore, the stronger their national identity the more affect they had towards the in-group. In terms of Catholic participants, strength of national identity was negatively correlated with affect and attitudes towards the traditional enemy (British). The stronger their national identity the less affect they had towards the traditional enemy and negative attitudes were present. SIDT proposes that at 7 years of age the child's focus moves away from the in-group and towards the out-groups where prejudice towards out-groups begins to emerge. This depends on the child's strength of subjective identification with the in-group (Nesdale, 2004, 2008). According to SIDT negative prejudice towards the "enemy" out-group is caused by the level of subjective identification with the in-group, how common negative attitudes are among the in-group, and the degree to which the in-group feels threatened by the out-group. According to Brewer (1999) a negative correlation between in-group and out-group evaluations may be present in "highly segmented societies that are differentiated along a single primary categorization, such as ethnicity or religion" when "the categorization is dichotomous, dividing the category into two significant subgroups" (p. 439). The present study found that development patterns varied between Catholic and Protestant children in terms of their affect and attitudes towards their own group and out-groups. Catholic participants rated their own group positively and evaluated the traditional enemy less positively than all other out-groups. In comparison Protestant children evaluated their own group positively and evaluated the German out-group less positively than all other groups. In a study by Barrett, Wilson, and Lyons (1999, 2003), when examining 5- to 11-year-old English children's trait attributions it was found that the children made the most positive attributes to the in-group (English) and the least positive attributes to the out-group (German). These findings could be the result of a wide range of factors. One explanation would be national enculturation where children have an attachment to a country's history, culture, traditions, etc. According to Barrett (2007) national enculturation can generate a sense of belonging and connection with one's own group. Children may have an emotional attachment to the history, culture and territory of their own country.

The findings from the present study can be further explained by social identity theory (SIT), in that in-group bias and out-group derogation could be a result of emotional attachment with one's own group. In societies where factors such as strong national identity, loyalty, sensitivity to threat and power politics are present a negative relationship may be found between in-group and out-group evaluations (Brewer, 1999). According to Hewstone, Rubin, and Willis (2002) the negative relationship between in-group and out-group evaluations may only occur in "situations of extreme intergroup conflict" (p. 579).

Societal-social-cognitive-motivational theory (SSCMT) explains that a child's national identity and attitudes towards in-group/out-group can be impacted by various factors, e.g., parental, teacher and peer group dialogue, etc. It is from all of these various sources that children can potentially acquire information about the pattern of relationships between their in-group and out-groups, and the relative status of their in-group within this broader structure of intergroup relations (Barrett, 2007). Young people in Northern Ireland have experienced the aftermath of the "Troubles" in a number of different ways especially indirectly through their family's experiences and reactions (Muldoon, Trew, & Kilpatrick, 2000).

Children and young people in post-conflict Northern Ireland provide hope for a peaceful future. A knowledge of children's national identity and intergroup attitudes and the impact they have upon each other is crucial if we want to make sure that the end of violence leads to the end of intergroup conflict.

REFERENCES

Amadeo, J., Torney-Purta, J., Lehmann, R., Husfeldt, V., & Nikolova, R. (2002). *Civic knowledge and engagement: An IEA study of upper secondary students in sixteen countries.* Amsterdam, The Netherlands: IEA.

Barrett, M. (2007). *Children's knowledge, beliefs and feelings about nations and national groups.* Hove, UK: Psychology Press.

Barrett, M., & Lyons, E. (2001, August). *National pride and the public collective self-esteem associated with the national group: A cross-national developmental analysis.* Paper presented at the Fourth INTAS Workshop. Uppsala University, Uppsala, Sweden.

Barrett, M., & Oppenheimer, L. (2011). Findings, theories and methods in the study of children's national identifications and national attitudes. *European Journal of Developmental Psychology, 8,* 5–24.

Barrett, M., Wilson, H., & Lyons, E. (1999). *Self-categorization theory and the development of national identity in English children.* Poster presented at the Biennial Meeting of the Society for Research in Child Development, Albuquerque, New Mexico, USA.

Barrett, M., Wilson, H., & Lyons, E. (2003). The development of national in-group bias: English children's attributions of characteristics to English, American and German people. *British Journal of Developmental Psychology, 21,* 193–220.

Brewer, M. B. (1999). The psychology of prejudice: In-group love or out-group hate? *Journal of Social Issues, 55,* 429–444.

Cairns, E. (1987). *Caught in crossfire.* Belfast, NI: Appletree Press.

Cairns, E. (2001). War, political violence and their psychological effects on children: Cultural concerns. *International Encyclopaedia of the Social and Behavioural Sciences* 2001, 16360 16363.

Cairns, E., & Cairns, T. (1995). Children and conflict: A psychological perspective. In S. Dunn (Ed.), *Facets of the conflict in Northern Ireland* (pp. 97–113). Basingstoke, UK: Macmillan.

Cairns, E., & Darby, J. (1998). The conflict in Northern Ireland; Causes, consequences and controls. *American Psychologist, 53,* 754–760.

Cairns, E., & Mercer, G. (1984). Social identity in Northern Ireland. *Human Relations, 37,* 1095–1102.

Cairns, E., Wilson, R., Gallagher, T., & Trew, K. (1995). Psychology's contribution to understanding conflict in Northern Ireland. *Peace and Conflict: Journal of Peace Psychology, 1,* 131–148.

Church, C., Visser, A., & Johnson, L. (2004). A path to peace or persistence? The "single identity" approach to conflict resolution in Northern Ireland. *Conflict Resolution Quarterly, 21,* 273–293.

Connolly, P., & Maginn, P. (1999). *Sectarianism, children and community relations in Northern Ireland.* Coleraine. UK: Centre for the Study of Conflict, University of Ulster.

Connolly, P., Smith, A., & Kelly, B. (2002). *Too young to notice? The cultural and political awareness of 3–6 year olds in Northern Ireland.* A report commissioned by the Northern Ireland Community Relations Council in Partnership with Channel 4.

Dennis, J., Lindberg, L., & McCrone, D. (1972). Support for nation and government among English children. *British Journal of Political Science, 1,* 25–48.

Devine, P., & Schubotz, D. (2004). *Us and them?* Young life and times research update, 28. (Available at www.ark.ac.uk/publications/updates/update28.pdf)

Gallagher, A. M. (1995). The approach of government: Community relations and equity. In S. Dunn (Ed.), *Facets of the conflict in Northern Ireland* (pp. 27–43). New York, NY: St. Martin's Press.

Gough, B., Robinson, S., Kremer, J., & Mitchell, R. (1992). The social psychology of intergroup conflict: An appraisal of Northern Ireland research. *Canadian Psychology, 33,* 645–650.

Hess, R. D., & Torney, J. V. (1967). *The development of political attitudes in children.* Chicago, IL: Aldine.

Hewstone, M., Cairns, E., Voci, A., Paolini, S., Mclernon, F., Crisp, R., et al. (2005). Intergroup contact in a divided society: Challenging segregation in Northern Ireland. In D. Abrams, J. M. Marques, & M. A. Hogg (Eds.), *The social psychology of inclusion and exclusion* (pp. 265–292). Philadelphia, PA: Psychology Press.

Hewstone, M., Rubin, M., & Willis, H. (2002). Intergroup bias. *Annual Review of Psychology, 53,* 575–604.

Hughes, J. (2003). Attitudes to community relations in Northern Ireland: Grounds for optimism? *Research Update,* No. 20.

Jahoda, G. (1962). Development of Scottish children's ideas and attitudes about other countries. *Journal of Social Psychology, 58,* 91–108.

Jaspers, J. M. F., Van de Geer, J. P., Tajfel, H., & Johnson, N. (1972). On the development of national attitudes in children. *European Journal of Social Psychology, 2,* 347–369.

Johnson, N. B., Middleton, M. R., & Tajfel, H. (1970). The relationship between children's preferences for and knowledge about other nations. *British Journal of Social and Clinical Psychology, 9,* 232–240.

Livingstone, A., & Haslam, S. A. (2008). The importance of social identity content in a setting of chronic social conflict: Understanding intergroup relations in Northern Ireland. *British Journal of Social Psychology, 47,* 1–21.

Middleton, M., Tajfel, H., & Johnson, N. B. (1970). Cognitive and affective aspects of children's national attitudes. *British Journal of Social and Clinical Psychology, 9,* 122–134.

Muldoon, O. T., Trew, K., & Kilpatrick, R. (2000). The legacy of the troubles on young people's psychological and social development and their school life. *Youth Society, 32,* 6–28.

Nesdale, D. (2004). Social identity processes and children's ethnic prejudice. In M. Bennett & F. Sani (Eds.), *The development of the social self* (pp. 219–245). Hove, UK: Psychology Press.

Nesdale, D. (2008). Social identity development and children's ethnic attitudes in Australia. In S. M. Quintana & C. McKown (Eds.), *The handbook of race, racism and the developing child* (pp. 313–338). Hoboken, NJ: Wiley.

Nugent, J. K. (1994). The development of children's relationships with their country. *Children's Environments, 11,* 281–291.

Reizábal, L., Valencia, J., & Barrett, M. (2004). National identifications and attitudes to national ingroups and outgroups among children living in the Basque Country. *Infant and Child Development, 13,* 1–20.

Tajfel, H. (1978). Social categorization, social identity and social comparison. In H. Tajfel (Ed.), *Differentiation between social groups: Studies in the social psychology of intergroup relations* (pp. 61–76). London, UK: Academic Press.

Tajfel, H., & Turner, J. C. (1979). An integrative theory of intergroup behaviour. In W. G. Austin & S. Worchel (Eds.), *The social psychology of intergroup relations* (pp. 33–48). Monterey, CA: Brooks/Cole.

Tajfel, H., & Turner, J. C. (1986). The social identity theory of intergroup behaviour. In S. Worchel & W. G. Austin (Eds.), *Psychology of intergroup relations* (2nd ed., pp. 7–24). Chicago, IL: Nelson-Hall.

Tausch, N., Hewstone, M., Kenworthy, J., Cairns, E., & Christ, O. (2007). Cross-community contact, perceived status differences and intergroup attitudes in Northern Ireland: The mediating roles of individual-level versus group-level threats and the moderating role of social identification. *Political Psychology, 28*, 53–68.

Teichman, Y., & Bar-Tal, D. (2008). Acquisition and development of a shared psychological intergroup repertoire in a context of intractable conflict. In S. M. Quintana & C. McKown (Eds.), *Handbook of race, racism, and the developing child* (pp. 452–482). New York, NY: Wiley.

Trew, K. (1986). Catholic–Protestant contact in Northern Ireland. In M. Hewstone & R. Brown (Eds.), *Contact and conflict in intergroup encounters* (pp. 93–106). Oxford, UK: Basil Blackwell.

Trew, K. (1992). Social psychological research on the conflict. *The Psychologist, 5*, 342–344.

Waddell, N., & Cairns, E. (1991). Identity preference in Northern Ireland. *Political Psychology, 12*, 205–213.

Whyte, J. (1990). *Interpreting Northern Ireland.* New York, NY: Oxford University Press.

EUROPEAN JOURNAL OF DEVELOPMENTAL PSYCHOLOGY
2011, 8 (1), 74–86

Ψ Psychology Press
Taylor & Francis Group

Children's perception of national identity and in-group/out-group attitudes: Turkish-Cypriot school children

Biran Mertan

Department of Psychology, Eastern Mediterranean University, Famagusta, North Cyprus

The aim of the current study was to explore the conceptual development of national identity in Turkish-Cypriot school children ranging from age 6 to 12. Cyprus presents a unique opportunity for the investigation of national identity and related issues due to its vibrant and unresolved political and historical milieu. Currently, there is no comprehensive developmental model that incorporates the conceptual development of national identity in children raised in stable political and national versus unstable political and national scenes. One would expect the sociopolitical environment in Cyprus to shape national identities that include large distances and enmities between the "self" and the "other". In total, 71 Turkish-Cypriot school children responded to the items of the National Identification Scale and were requested to indicate their liking for in-group and out-group targets as well as the appropriateness of traits to describe the in-group and out-groups. In order to provide bases for comparisons between the in-group (Turkish Cypriots) and the enemy out-group (Greek Cypriots), two neutral out-groups (Ireland and the Netherlands) were also used as target groups. The present data suggest that while age has no impact, gender does have an impact on the development of national identity. In the current sample girls demonstrated higher national identity than boys. Data also indicated strong in-group favouritism and negativity towards the enemy out-group.

Keywords: Turkish-Cypriot children; National identity; Political and historical milieu; Conceptual development.

Correspondence should be addressed to Biran Mertan, Department of Psychology, Eastern Mediterranean University, Famagusta, North Cyprus, Mersin 10, Turkey.
E-mail: biran.mertan@emu.edu.tr

© 2011 Psychology Press, an imprint of the Taylor & Francis Group, an Informa business
http://www.psypress.com/edp   DOI: 10.1080/17405629.2010.533982

INTRODUCTION

The question of how children develop the concept of national identity and attitudes towards members of the in-group and out-group has been the topic of considerable research over the last three decades (see Barrett, 2007, for a review). Despite this highly dynamic research area, there is a lack of a comprehensive developmental model that clearly explains national identity and attitudes towards in-group and out-group.

Literature regarding national identity and in-group/out-group attitudes in children is well documented in the social and developmental literature. However, the role of sociohistorical settings in the development of national identity and in-group/out-group attitudes in children has not been thoroughly examined. The present research addresses this issue. One would expect that properties of sociohistorical settings shape children's perceptions of identity and their in-group/out-group attitudes and that conjectural changes will lead to fluctuations in perceptions and attitudes. As suggested by Teichman and Bar-Tal (2008) intractable conflicts between political, cultural, or ethnic groups affect all society members including children. We therefore believe that recent sociohistorical developments in Cyprus such as 50 years of conflicts provide a good context in which to look at perceptions of national identity and "us" and "them" categorizations.

The following is a brief description of the state of affairs in Cyprus in order for the reader to appreciate the complexities faced by the Cypriots, in particular children. Cyprus is an Eastern Mediterranean island and a former British colony, which gained its independence and became an autonomous state in 1960. Although, the Greek and Turkish Cypriots have had a history of coexistence in mixed villages and towns, Cypriots have never had a common language to communicate. In their private domains members of each community used their own native language (e.g., Greek, Turkish, Armenian, Maronite or Latin). Turkish and Greek, as it was stated in article 3 of the Cyprus Constitution, were the official languages of the Republic of Cyprus. These two languages were also used on currency and stamps along with the English language. The colonial heritage in Cyprus was manifest in all aspects of life including education, where both Turkish and Greek Cypriot school children had to sing the British national anthem.

The Republic of Cyprus, as a sovereign state, had essentially two major communities, Greek Cypriots and Turkish Cypriots. Each of the communities not only spoke different languages but also practised different religions (i.e., Orthodox Christians vs. Moslems, respectively). The only emblem that Cypriots had in common was the neutrally designed and coloured Cypriot flag, a conventionally agreed upon emblem representing the Republic of Cyprus. However, under the laws of the Republic, the Cypriot flag with all rights could only be flown beside the Greek or Turkish flags. The Turkish and Greek flags symbolized trust to the "motherlands". As it was stated in articles 1 and 2 of the Constitution of Republic of Cyprus, the State of Cyprus was composed of two main communities, Greek and Turkish that are affiliated with their Greek and Turkish origins and languages (i.e., Greek and Turkish).

As a result of close relations with and loyalty towards their "motherlands", it did not take long for problems and conflicts to arise based on identity and security needs. Nationalist narratives and movements in both communities led to hostilities and enmities against each other as in-group versus out-group, and finally resulted in a war and regional separation of the two communities. Numerous international attempts during the past three decades to solve the conflict, bring peace and establish security on the island, have persistently failed.

The long period of friction between the two communities on the island reinforced a more powerful awareness and loyalty to ethnicity based identities (i.e., "Turkish Cypriotness" and "Greek Cypriotness"). The symbols and emblems of each community as well as their rituals and ceremonials played important roles in mediating and sustaining the "Turkish Cypriot" and "Greek Cypriot" identities and in creating a large distance between perceptions of the "self" and the "other". As suggested by Barrett (2007), these symbols and emblems provided perceptible salient markers with which group members could identify in the course of their everyday lives. In this sociopolitical environment, family and school practices both in the Turkish- and Greek-Cypriot communities supported ethnic identities and reinforced antagonism against each other. Children were systematically exposed to over-exaggerated ethnocentric historical narratives and cultural heritage. For example, every day Turkish-Cypriot school children had to stand in front of Atatürk's bust and recite the pledge of allegiance both to the Turkish flag and Turkish motherland. In school, history books included narratives to enforce ethno-national and religious identities and derogate the "other". After the 1960s many generations have grown up in school and home environments that stigmatized the "other" and described the other as the "enemy". Turkish Cypriots born after 1974, when Turkey intervened because of a coup d'état to annex the island to Greece by EOKA (i.e., the National Organization of Cypriot Fighters), were particularly susceptible to such indoctrination because they did not have any opportunity for direct contact with Greek Cypriots at all. As an example of distancing the "other" from the "self", the Turkish word " gavur " that is differentially defined as enemy, non-Muslim, Christian, infidel, unbeliever, merciless, cruel, heartless or obstinate became the popular adjective to designate the "others", namely the Greek Cypriots, Armenians, Latinos, and Maronites cohabiting on the island of Cyprus. Similar practices were not rare for Greek-Cypriot children.

During the last decades, national identity cards for Turkish Cypriots have changed three times in response to political negotiations and changes in

Cyprus, while Greek Cypriots have retained the same identity cards. These changes took place not only on paper for Turkish Cypriots, but also psychologically. For example, North Cyprus went from being an "Autonomous Turkish State" to a "Turkish Federated State" to, now, a "Turkish Republic of Northern Cyprus". Throughout this process, each label had distinct political and psychological repercussion for Turkish Cypriots.

Long-term negotiations in order to bring peace to the island have recently resulted in only controlled mobility between the South and the North. From April 2003, native Turkish Cypriots living in the North can visit the South and Greek Cypriots can visit the North. Also from that date, Turkish-Cypriot authorities have started to change history schoolbooks and to eliminate narratives and historical events that strengthen ethnic identity and hostility against the other. Instead, the new textbooks incorporate elements emphasizing "Cypriotness", "togetherness", friendship, and co-operation. Similar attempts are being made by the Greek-Cypriot authorities. However, such changes will require time to yield the desired outcomes. Therefore, in this study we expected that the teachings in the second half of the twentieth century in this conflict area would prevail and hypothesized that Turkish-Cypriot school children aged 7 and 11 would still show a strong national identification and that this identification would be stronger in older children. In addition, these children were expected to evaluate the in-group (i.e., the Turkish Cypriots) more positively than the out-group (i.e., the Greek Cypriots) demonstrating in-group favouritism. Moreover the difference between in-group/out-group attitudes was expected to be higher for the older children. Finally, stronger national identification was expected to be associated with a higher degree of differentiation between the in-group and the out-group.

METHOD

Participants

The participants were 71 Turkish-Cypriot children (38 boys and 33 girls) consisting of two age groups with mean ages 7.20 (i.e., the 7-year-olds; $SD = 0.76$, $n = 39$) and 11.23 (i.e., the 11-year-olds; $SD = 0.65$, $n = 32$). The sample was accessed using a snowball strategy in public and private schools in North Cyprus. All children came from native Turkish-Cypriot families.

Materials and procedure

The data were collected using a Turkish version of Barrett's Strength of Identification Scale (SoIS; 2007) and a trait attribution task and affect questions (Barrett et al., 1997). The SoIS has six subscales, namely: affect towards national identity; positive internalization of national identity; negative internalization of national identity; degree of identification; importance of national identity; and national pride, each represented by a single item. A rating scale accompanies each item. In the trait attribution task, twelve positive and negative trait words were used to assess in- and out-group attributions. The positive traits were clean, friendly, clever, happy, honest, and hardworking, and the negative ones were dirty, unfriendly, stupid, lazy, sad, and dishonest. Each child picked as many traits as she/he thought described the target group. In response to the affect questions, the child indicated their liking for the in-group and each of the out-groups on a scale running from 5 (*like very much*) to 1 (*dislike very much*). In order to provide a basis for comparison between attitudes to the in-group (Turkish Cypriots) and attitudes to the enemy out-group (Greek Cypriots), two neutral out-groups (Ireland and the Netherlands) were also used as target groups. All materials were translated into Turkish and back translated to English by two researchers from the field of psychology fluent in both the Turkish and English languages. For full details of all the tasks and the procedures that were employed in their administration, see Barrett and Oppenheimer (2011 this issue).

The data were collected in 2006, two years after Cyprus had become a member of the European Union, excluding North Cyprus since it had declared its independence in 1983. A week prior to data collection, letters were sent to the parents of children informing them of the project and giving them the option of declining participation of their son or daughter. Among those contacted, only one child was dropped from the sample because the parents did not approve of their child's participation. The instrument used in data collection was administered either in the home or school environment in a face-to-face situation. Each child was reassured that they were not being tested and that there were no right or wrong answers.

RESULTS

National Identification

Responses to the items of the National Identification Scale constituted measures of children's perception of dimensions of national identification (i.e., degree of national identification, affect towards national identity, internalization of national identity, importance of national identity and national pride). Table 1 shows the means and standard deviations for each dimension of national identification for each age group and gender.

As can be seen in this table, younger children did not differ from the older ones in expressing their national identity. Indeed, an analysis of covariance

TABLE 1
Mean scores (and standard deviations) for the dimensions of National Identification for each age and gender

| | Age | | | | | |
| | 7-years (n = 39) | | | 11-years (n = 32) | | |
NI-aspects	Boy	Girl	Total	Boy	Girl	Total
Degree	4.05 (1.14)	4.29 (1.13)	4.18 (1.14)	4.35 (0.85)	5.00 (0.00)	4.62 (0.69)
Affect	4.61 (0.63)	4.70 (1.03)	4.65 (0.86)	4.21 (0.70)	4.67 (0.67)	4.38 (0.70)
NegInt	4.17 (0.74)	3.95 (1.30)	4.05 (1.07)	4.20 (1.06)	4.58 (0.50)	4.34 (0.89)
PosInt	4.67 (0.49)	4.38 (0.62)	4.51 (0.56)	4.65 (0.49)	4.83 (0.40)	4.72 (0.45)
Importance	3.88 (1.59)	4.72 (0.54)	4.33 (1.22)	4.11 (1.09)	4.41 (0.73)	4.23 (0.94)
Pride	4.24 (1.22)	4.71 (0.73)	4.48 (0.99)	4.20 (1.31)	4.65 (0.65)	4.36 (1.08)

Note: PosInt = Positive Internalization; NegInt = Negative Internalization.

(ANCOVA) with Gender and the Identification Dimensions as within factors and age as a covariate resulted in only a significant main effect for Gender, $F(1, 59) = 5.90$, $p < .02$. Girls overall identity average score ($M = 4.60$) was higher than the average for boys ($M = 4.30$).

A reliability analysis with the six dimensions of national identification resulted in a Cronbach's alpha of .54, which is not rare when the number of items is small. An exploratory principal component analysis with varimax rotation indicated that negative internalization did not contribute significantly to children's perceptions of national identity. In Figure 1, the factor loadings of the dimensions together with their means and intercorrelations are presented. As shown in the figure, the largest contribution came from pride of one's own identity (loading = .74) followed by degree of identification (loading = .68).

The dimension of negative internalization was not related to children's identity perceptions or correlated with other dimensions except positive internalization ($r = .29$, $p < .05$). As Figure 1 shows, being proud of one's own national identity had significant correlations with the dimensions of affect ($r = .36$), degree ($r = .33$), and importance ($r = .37$). In Figure 1, the mean scores for each dimension of national identification are also shown, which were high and ranged from 4.18 to 4.61.

In-group/out-group attitudes

Attitudes of Turkish-Cypriot children towards the in-group and the out-groups were assessed by the trait attributions and a like–dislike measure. A multivariate analysis of variance (MANOVA) employing Gender as between and Domain (positive–negative) and Target Group (in-group,

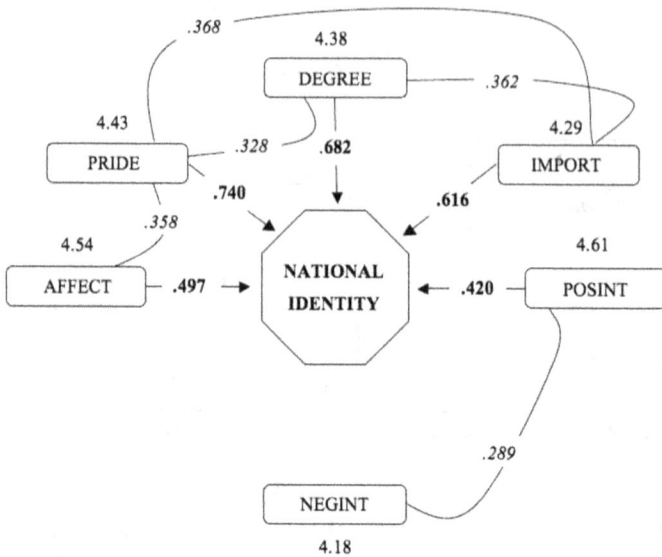

Figure 1. A schematic representation of the one-factor structure of National Identification, showing the factor loadings for (**bold**) the mean scores of, and the correlations (*italics*) among the dimensions of national identification for the Turkish-Cypriot children.

enemy out-group, and two neutral out-groups) as within factors and age as covariate resulted only in significant main effects for the Domain, $F(1, 69) = 45.57$, $p < .001$, and Target Group, $F(3, 207) = 18.49$, $p < .001$. The interaction was also significant, $F(1, 207) = 7.87$, $p < .01$.

In Table 2, the mean number of positive and negative attributes are presented that were judged to best describe the in- and out-groups. The means in the table indicate strong in-group favouritism on the positive traits. The mean for the in-group was significantly different than the means for the enemy out-group, $t(70) = 8.53$, $p < .001$, and the means for the two

TABLE 2
Trait attributions according to domain and target group

Target group	Domain	
	Positive trait	Negative trait
In-group	3.16	0.51
Enemy out-group	1.14	1.67
Neutral out-group 1	1.60	0.78
Neutral out-group 2	1.73	0.66

neutral groups, $t(70) = 7.41$, and $t(70) = 5.99$, both with $p < .001$. The mean numbers of positive traits judged to be descriptive of the two neutral groups were also significantly higher than the mean number of positive adjectives for the enemy group, $t(70) = 1.94$, $p < .06$, and $t(70) = 2.91$, $p < .005$, in that order.

The data in Table 2 further reveals that the mean number of negative traits attributed to the in-group was the smallest, the difference between this mean and the mean for the enemy group was significant, $t(70) = 5.20$, $p < .001$.

Children did not differentiate between the in-group and the neutral out-groups, but judged the enemy group as having significantly more negative traits than the neutral out-groups (with t-values being 4.37 and 4.96, both being significant at $\alpha = .001$).

As with trait attributions, the ANCOVA on the like–dislike measure did not reveal main and interaction effects for age and gender. The data were subjected to a one-way repeated-measures ANOVA. This analysis yielded significant differences in children's liking for the in-group and the out-groups, $F(3, 192) = 43.96$, $p < .001$. Children liked the in-group most ($M = 4.88$), and the enemy out-group the least ($M = 2.78$). The mean likings for the neutral out-groups were 3.45 for the Irish and 3.68 for Dutch. The in-group average was significantly higher than the averages for the out-groups, the t-values ranging from 7.70 to 10.48. The neutral out-groups were evaluated more positively than the enemy out-group, $t(70) = 3.14$ and $t(70) = 4.20$ ($\alpha = .005$). There was no significant difference in children's liking for the Irish and Dutch out-groups, $t(70) = 1.87$, $p < .07$.

Relationships between identity components and trait attributions and liking

Correlation analysis indicated that identity components did not relate to trait attributions and to liking for the out-groups. Excluding negative and positive internalization components, weak to moderate correlations were obtained between the other components of national identity and liking for the in-group. Table 3 indicates the correlation coefficients among identity components and liking for the in-group and the out-groups. As can be seen in the table, identity components did not relate to liking for the enemy out-group, where unexpected negative correlations occurred between liking for the two neutral out-groups and two of the dimensions of National Identification, that is, affect and positive internalization of national identity. Correlations of identity components with positive and negative trait attributions for the target groups were very similar to the correlations of those components with liking, and therefore they are not reported here.

TABLE 3
Correlation coefficients among identity components and liking for
in-group and out-groups

Identitfication dimensions	In-group	Enemy out-group	Neutral out-group 1	Neutral out-group 2
Degree	.26**	.20	−.01	−.04
Affect	.38**	.02	−.30*	−.24*
NegInt	.02	.05	−.16	−.11
PosInt	.03	−.15	−.34**	−.36**
Importance	.39**	.13	−.05	.02
Pride	.36	.12	.00	−.03

Note: *$\alpha = .05$, two tailed; **$\alpha = .01$, two tailed.

DISCUSSION

The current study addressed the issue of Turkish-Cypriot children's perception of national identity in a group of 7- to 11-year-old children. Turkish-Cypriot children's national identity perceptions were very strong. The scores on the six dimensions of National Identification were all high and close to the highest possible scale value. Apparently protracted conflict and dispute between population groups or communities create a sociopsychological context that strengthens in-group perceptions. Indeed, the very high scores for the positive internalization, affect toward national identity, and national pride are indicative of a strong need to stick to national values and identities in expressing and describing the self.

Our findings with respect to the strength of the dimensions of National Identification among Turkish-Cypriot children is consistent with the findings of an earlier study with adult Turkish Cypriots reported by Vural and Rustemli (2006). Like adults, Turkish-Cypriot children internalize the official (i.e., collective) conceptualization of their ethnic background (i.e., of being Turkish). Due to the unresolved political situation in Cyprus, Turkish-Cypriot children are arguably more exposed to nationalistic discourse as compared to children in politically stable settings. As suggested by Appadurai (1990) one of the underlying reasons could be the *mediascapes* leading to a large complex repertoire of nationalist images and related narratives by the media. In this way the media present a nationalism that has to lead to the triumph of the Turkish nation and that incites Turkish-Cypriot children to be proud of their national identity.

In this study, age differences were predicted between younger and older children in their perceptions of national identity in favour of the older age group. No support for this prediction was found. One possible explanation for the absence of an age effect on National Identification might be the age range sampled in this study. The present sample consisted of school children ranging in age from 6 to 12. Nesdale, Maass, Griffiths, and Durkin (2003) suggested that the development of national identity occurs in sequential stages the last of which is the stage of "ethnic preference" that appears around age 7. In the present study, all children were probably at this last developmental stage and exhibiting strong identification with "Turkishness" or "Turkish Cypriotness". Therefore, the saturation of the present sample does not offer insights into the development of National Identification in environments where intergroup disputes and conflicts prevail for long periods of time as compared to its development in environments where peace and order prevail.

Whereas no gender differences were expected, on most dimensions of National Identification girls scored higher than boys. The stronger identification of girls as Turkish Cypriots may be due to their closer and more frequent exposure to family narratives from older female members. As Lyons (2007) pointed out the emotional remembering and the narratives of suffering for Turkish Cypriots are an important medium for both personal and collective engagement. Actually, girls identified themselves completely with "Turkish Cypriots" and are highly sensitive to positive opinions about their nation (i.e., positive internalization). Majob and Abdo (2004) discussed the societal investment of women with cultural values as "reproductors" of the nation. Girls themselves may also be internalizing this role. Hence, compared to boys, girls may perceive themselves more vulnerable to political conflicts and instability on the island and thus internalize in-group values and identities more strongly than boys. To examine this gender difference in National Identification among Turkish-Cypriot children further research is required.

The conceptualization of a sense of belonging to their nation for Turkish-Cypriot children is not a singular but a composite construct related to "Turkish Cypriotness". That is, when children are asked to rate their national identity, a clear pattern emerges involving national symbols such as flags that concurrently refer to the Turkish and Turkish-Cypriot nations. Ideally one should evaluate "Turkishness", "Cypriotness" and "Turkish Cypriotness" separately before drawing firm conclusions, because Turkish-Cypriot children grow up in a national context in which "Cypriotness" and "Turkishness" both prevail together.

One may question the strength of the children's subjective identification with their own national and state in-group when raised in a society that is subject to the transformation of collective identity. Following the geographic and political separation of the island in 1974, traditional ethnic identities were exploited by official discourse in both the Greek- and Turkish-Cypriot communities strengthening the distance between the "other" and the "self". As suggested by Anastasiou (2007), social and political discourse sustains the conflict and constructs a reality of irresolvable problems. Therefore, for each community the conflict in Cyprus has become part of the identity of the country. To examine in-group/out-group comparisons with Turkish-Cypriot children who grow up in this politically conflicting environment, attitudes towards the in-group and the out-groups were assessed by trait attribution and a like–dislike measure.

As was expected, Turkish-Cypriot children demonstrated a strong in-group favouritism toward their own national group. The Turkish-Cypriot community (i.e., nation) was judged considerably more positively (i.e., obtained more positive adjectives) than the two neutral out-groups (i.e., Ireland and the Netherlands) and the traditional enemy out-group (i.e., Greek Cypriots). In addition, the Greek Cypriots were more negatively evaluated than the in-group as well as the two neutral out-groups. Overall, children's positive evaluations of the in- and out-groups exceeded their negative evaluations of all evaluated groups. This finding may reflect the presently more stable status with no physical violence among the two nations in the country (i.e., as a result of the UN ceasefire since 1974) despite the fact that the political conflict in Cyprus is still unresolved and an official peace treaty has yet to be signed.

In the literature on children's attitudes towards their own in-group no consistent developmental patterns were evident. In the present study, clear in-group favouritism was observed with the Turkish-Cypriot children. Of interest here is that while children positively relate to their own national identity by being Turkish Cypriot, the strength of their National Identification is negatively related to their affect towards Greek Cypriots (i.e., the traditional enemy). These findings are consistent with social identity theory (Tajfel & Turner, 1986), in which it is predicted that children's intergroup attitudes will be affected by knowledge of the prevailing structure of intergroup relations within which their own group is embedded.

Although the children involved in the study have only been exposed to a very limited part of the historical events that took place on the island, they have nevertheless been subject to a bombardment of ethnocentric curricula involving out-group derogation and national pride in their formal and informal education. Through selective, exaggerated, and often false, memories of adults in their environment, children develop a mono-focal and biased understanding of reality. The political and historical dilemmas in which these children mature define their identities, which are often confused, and how they view themselves vis à vis these events. Recently, Turkish Cypriots voted positively for the Annan Plan (i.e., a UN plan for the solution of the Cyprus problem) in a referendum on April 2004. With a vote of 65% in favour of the plan, the Turkish Cypriots showed impressive support for the Annan Plan and demonstrated the strength of their national identity and reduced negative attitudes towards Greek Cypriots. On the other hand, it is not rare to see that Turkish-Cypriot children living in a traditional-amalgam family structure (Mertan, 2003) are exposed to fluctuations between different inter-generational national identities (Vural & Rustemli, 2006).

In the context of Cyprus, the formation of national identity as a dynamic psychological construct is different for Turkish and Greek Cypriots. While for both groups the main sociohistorical elements are common (i.e., civic Cypriotness), other elements such as ethno-national (Turkishness vs. Greekness), religious (Moslemness vs. Orthodox Christianity) and linguistic (Turkish vs. Greek) are different. Because no Cypriot language exists, and language is considered to be one of the most important components of a culture (i.e., nation), no common and shared understanding by the Turkish- and Greek-Cypriot communities could be developed for the resolution of the situation in Cyprus. As a consequence, the English language (i.e., a third language) is presently used by the majority of Cypriots for intergroup communication.

The sense of belonging to "Turkish Cypriotness" for the Turkish-Cypriot school children is dependent on contextual variables such as the media, political discourse, close inter-generational relations and parental practices, and the educational system, including teachers, peers, curricula, and textbooks. All these variables and more constitute multiple factors that influence the development of children's national identity and ethnic-group attitudes. In addition, Turkish Cypriot children live in a society that struggles internationally to be recognized as a distinct Turkish Cypriot group. This struggle functions as a diffuse yet constant threat that may serve to strengthen Turkish Cypriot children's national identities. Unlike their peers in countries that are politically well established, Turkish Cypriot children do not have the psychological freedom to allow their sense of national identity to fluctuate. Because their context is not settled, their national identity becomes rigid. In Cypriot school children's everyday vibrant and unresolved political milieu, Cypriot identity and power sharing between two communities are becoming the banalities of political discourse. The development of Turkish-Cypriot children's national identity as "Turkish Cypriot" would then be a consequence of composite conventional ethnic motivations to become superior to Greek Cypriots and to keep strong ties with the superordinate identity of Turkishness.

REFERENCES

Anastasiou, M. (2007). *The institutionalization of protracted ethnic conflicts: A discourse analysis of "the Cyprus Problem"*. Unpublished doctoral dissertation, University of South Carolina, Columbia, SC, USA.

Appadurai, A. (1990). Disjuncture and difference in the global cultural economy. *Theory, Culture, and Society, 7*, 295–310.

Barrett, M. (2007). *Children's knowledge, beliefs and feelings about nations and national groups.* Hove, UK: Psychology Press.

Barrett, M., Lyons, E., Bennett, M., Vila, I., Giménez, A., Arcuri, L., et al. (1997). *Children's beliefs and feelings about their own and other national groups in Europe.* Final Report to the Commission of the European Communities, Directorate-General XII for Science, Research and Development, Human Capital and Mobility (HCM) Programme, Research Network No. CHRX-CT94–0687.

Barrett, M., & Oppenheimer, L. (2011). Findings, theories and methods in the study of children's national identifications and national attitudes. *European Journal of Developmental Psychology, 8,* 5–24.

Lyons, B. E. (2007). *Narratives of suffering, dynamics of space and practices of intergenerational memory in Turkish Cyprus.* Unpublished doctoral dissertation, University of California, Los Angeles, CA, USA.

Majob, S., & Abdo, N. (2004). *Violence in the name of honour. The theoretical and political challenges.* Istanbul, Turkey: Bilgi University Press.

Mertan, B. (2003). Social and emotional development of Turkish Cypriot children and caregiving styles. *Woman 2000, Journal For Woman Studies EMU-CWS, 3*(2), 1–16.

Nesdale, D., Maass, A., Griffiths, J., & Durkin, K. (2003). Effects of ingroup and outgroup ethnicity on children's attitudes towards members of the ingroup and outgroup. *British Journal of Developmental Psychology, 21,* 177–192.

Tajfel, H., & Turner, J. C. (1986). The social identity theory of intergroup behaviour. In S. Worchel & W. G. Austin (Eds.), *Psychology of intergroup relations* (2nd ed., pp. 7–24). Chicago, IL: Nelson-Hall.

Teichman, Y., & Bar-Tal, D. (2008). Acquisition and development of a shared psychological intergroup repertoire in a context of an intractable conflict. In S. M. Quintana & C. McKown (Eds.), *Handbook of race, racism, and the developing child* (pp. 452–482). Hoboken, NJ: Wiley.

Vural, Y., & Rustemli, A. (2006). Identity fluctuations in the Turkish Cypriot community. *Mediterranean Politics, 11,* 329–348.

EUROPEAN JOURNAL OF DEVELOPMENTAL PSYCHOLOGY
2011, 8 (1), 87–97

Ψ Psychology Press
Taylor & Francis Group

National identity and in-group/out-group attitudes with Greek-Cypriot children

Panayiotis Stavrinides and Stelios Georgiou

Department of Psychology, University of Cyprus, Nicosia, South Cyprus

The primary purpose of this study is to examine the relationship between the internalization of national identity and in-group/out-group attitudes among Greek-Cypriot children. We also aimed to investigate whether the internalization of national identity develops as a single/unified construct, or is manifested as the result of independent dimensions (i.e., national pride, degree of internalization, affect towards national group, etc.). Moreover, we examine whether the degree of national identity and "enemy images" (i.e., out-group stereotypes) are dependent on age and gender. In the present study, the participants were 75 Greek-Cypriot children, 40 boys and 35 girls with mean age of 10.03 years. The participants were divided into two age groups; younger group ($n = 18$) and older group ($n = 57$) with a mean age of 6.95 years for the younger group and 11.00 years for the older group. The results provide evidence against the thesis that the internalization of national identity in Greek-Cypriot children is a unified and consistent construct. In fact, internal consistency analysis reveals that each dimension of national identity is relatively independent. Further analyses show that none of the aspects of national identity correlate significantly with either positive or negative out-group attitudes. The internalization of national pride, however, shows a significant positive correlation with in-group positive bias. Accordingly, national pride and a positive internalization of national identity are negatively correlated with negative in-group attitudes. Age and gender comparisons reveal that girls show significantly higher scores on the importance of national identity subscale, and there is also a significant age by gender interaction on the same subscale showing that older boys have higher scores than younger boys but younger girls have significantly higher scores than older girls. The results of our study are discussed in relation to the sociocultural context of Greek-Cypriot society and the effects of the collective conflict experiences in the development of enemy images in childhood.

Keywords: National identification; Greek-Cypriot children; In-group/out-group attitudes.

Correspondence should be addressed to Panayiotis Stavrinides, Department of Psychology, University of Cyprus, P.O. Box 20537, 1678, Nicosia, South Cyprus. E-mail: stavrini@ucy.ac.cy

© 2011 Psychology Press, an imprint of the Taylor & Francis Group, an Informa business
http://www.psypress.com/edp   DOI: 10.1080/17405629.2010.533989

INTRODUCTION

Sociohistorical context: The case of Greek Cypriots

The Greek-Cypriot society has always been Hellenocentric. Even though the Republic of Cyprus emerged as an independent state in 1960 (see Panteli, 1990), a large part of the Greek-Cypriot community has never moved from the Hellenocentric ideology to a more inclusive Cyprocentric one (Mavratsas, 1998). The previously uniform demand for *enosis* (unification) with Greece, even if it could not be achieved, remained an unfulfilled vision for many Greek Cypriots. Both at the institutional and at the societal level, a significant number of people kept the belief that Cyprus should be united with the "motherland" and that Turkish Cypriots as a minority should accept that fact and exercise their individual rights within a Greek province. Despite the fact that Cyprus as an independent and bicommunal state was developing the capacity to function within the international community detached from the influences of the past—either the colonial or the demand for *enosis*—the unfulfilled goal was guiding many of the actions of the Greek Cypriots.

In other words, the Greek-Cypriot community during the first years of the independence, instead of emphasizing how the newly formed state would become the common homeland for Greek Cypriots and Turkish Cypriots, focused on how to promote its Greek heritage that separated the community from its Turkish-Cypriot compatriots. Even though the two communities shared the geographical boundaries of the island, they mostly kept their communities apart from each other. The villages and towns remained either predominantly Greek or Turkish, families were composed of either Greek only or Turkish only members, and even some professions were predominantly occupied by either Greek or Turkish people (Patrick, 1976). Peaceful coexistence on the island was essentially kept for only three years after independence, and soon the separationist and conflict climate was predominant within the country.

For more than four decades now, the two communities have been geographically, socially, economically, and psychologically separated. This division is expressed in various ways, but it becomes much more obvious and explicit when it comes to the educational system. The Hellenocentrism of the educational system in the Greek-Cypriot society has operated for decades not only as a barrier towards the Turkish-Cypriot community but also as the cultivator of a non-tolerant approach towards the out-group, and has promoted the concept of the enemy as part of what anything labelled as Turkish might represent. That may be Turkey as a country, the Turkish people, and the Turkish Cypriots.

At the symbolic level, many of the school rituals and ceremonies have remained Greek centred. Greek-Cypriot schools celebrate every Greek national holiday, the national anthem of Greece is sung at the school celebrations and events, and the Greek flag is placed in every public school. During the major Greek national holidays, the students perform parades to celebrate national events such as the Greek revolution against the Ottoman empire of 1821 and the more recent resistance to Mussolini's Italy of 1940.

At the more pragmatic level, much of the curriculum is based on the so-called Helleno-Christian ideals. Greek-Cypriot students at all levels of their primary and secondary education are expected to attend classes of religious studies, which are basically a promotion of the Greek-Orthodox doctrine, and a prayer is recited every morning before classes commence. History as it is taught does not allow any critical approach to various events, neither does it allow any space for alternative explanations of historical incidents. In many chapters of the history texts, Hellenocentrism and in-group favouritism is not only explicit but, more worryingly, it is expected by the students as the conventional approach. In general, at all major historical eras, Greece and its people represent virtue and morality while all the opposing people are labelled as uncivilized and barbaric. Not surprisingly, during the 2004 referendum for the proposed solution of the Cyprus issue, students of all ages rallied against the endorsement of the United Nations proposal (Portides & Stavrinides, 2008).

Undoubtedly, the war of 1974 has been the most traumatic event in the recent history of the Greek Cypriots. Many lives were lost, a significant number of Greek Cypriots have been missing ever since, and approximately one third of the population was displaced. This has created a stronger sense of self-justification within the Greek-Cypriot society that uniformly represents the in-group as the victim and the out-group as the aggressor (Papadakis, 1993). Turkey, the Turkish people as a whole, and Turkish Cypriots are many times represented as a unified schema of evilness and animosity that elicits fear (Stavrinides, 2009). Such diffusion has been passed on for the last three and a half decades and education has assumed the role of maintaining the collective representations of Greek-Cypriot victimization and Turkish aggression. Preschool education, as an earlier stage of the formal school years, also appears to play a significant role, especially in cultivating the grounds of young children's frames of mind. Stories, myths, and legends are often told with reference to the victimization of the Greek Cypriots and the atrocities of the Turks. Children by the age of five have already been taught how to sing the Greek national anthem, and on Greek national holidays they perform plays and songs with patriotic (and in some instances nationalistic) references.

Military service is mandatory for all male youths immediately after they graduate from high school. During the 25-month period of their service, young men (most of them still adolescents) receive an explicit form of military training, they are equipped with weapons, and they are instructed how to perform in military battles against the enemy, which of course is Turkey and the north of Cyprus. During this period in their late teens, which is critical for identity formation, Greek-Cypriot youths are formally taught hate against anything Turkish and they prepare themselves to take away lives of Turkish Cypriots if that will serve the greater and so-called noble cause for justice and liberty.

Greek-Cypriot society has developed over the past four decades in a way that promotes the transference of beliefs and attitudes about the traditional enemy. This has taken place across all levels of the society and its impact can be observed across all ages starting with childhood. Parents and grand-parents, as significant socialization agents, often play the role of instructors in this process of out-group demonization and the development of the enemy concept in their children. In popular culture and discourse, it is frequently observed that Turks are portrayed as the equivalent of evil (Papadakis, 1993).

Parents try to pass moral lessons on to their children by narrating stories in which the Turks represent everything that is immoral, while Greeks, on the other hand, become archetypal figures of kindness, morality, and virtue. Today's grandparents represent the generation with direct experience of the 1974 conflict. Not surprisingly, it is implicitly expected of them to pass on their experiences of those days. Even though nobody questions whether such experiences were traumatic and their effects were dramatic and long standing, the oral tradition is mostly narrated in a way that always expresses the victimization of the Greek Cypriots and the atrocities of the Turks. Fortunately, however, this description does not fit all the family patterns that are observed in Greek-Cypriot society, even though it represents a predominant pattern of child-rearing practices.

Currently, the Greek-Cypriot ministry of education is making a concerted effort to promote reconciliation and coexistence between the two communities on the island. This policy, however, is met with a great deal of scepticism and rejection. In its yearly address to the educational community, the ministry of education has placed as its primary targets for the present academic year the promotion in our schools of the ideals of reconciliation, mutual understanding, and peaceful coexistence between the Greek Cypriots and the Turkish Cypriots. As a reaction to this address, the teachers' unions of primary and secondary education, a number of political parties, the church, and a significant part of the media reacted by rejecting the ministry's policy and calling upon the minister to withdraw his intended policy.

Contrary to the ministry's declared policy, many of the institutions that reacted in such a way have proposed that the Hellenocentric type of education should be promoted instead, with an emphasis on the development of the Greek-Orthodox national identity in Greek-Cypriot children.

The conclusion from the above is that we assume that young children in Greek-Cypriot society, from an early period in their development, create a crystallized concept or image of an enemy, which is represented within a generalized schema of anything Turkish (Turkey, Turkish people, and Turkish Cypriots). This conceptual development must be related to a significantly high level of in-group favouritism and an equally high level of out-group negative attitudes (Bar-Tal, & Teichman, 2005; Bennett, Lyons, Sani, & Barrett, 1998; Bigler, Brown, & Markell, 2001; Bigler, Jones, & Lobliner, 1997; Nesdale & Flesser, 2001; Poppe & Linssen, 1999; Rutland, 1999; Teichman, 2001; Teichman, & Bar-Tal, 2008), particularly when the out-group represents the enemy concept. Along with that, we expect that the internalization of the national identity will be well structured and at significantly high levels (Barrett, 2007; Bennett et al., 2004).

The present study

The sociohistorical setting of Greek-Cypriot society raises a number of questions that are addressed in the present study. Is internalization of the national identity in Greek-Cypriot children a single/unified construct? If this is the case, then it is expected that the dimensions of national identity such as national pride, the degree of internalization, and affect towards one's own national group will be significantly correlated and load onto a single latent construct.

Another important question has to do with the relation of national identification with other cognitive and affective factors. For example, does the internalization of national identity in Greek-Cypriot children correlate with either (a) in-group favouritism or (b) out-group (Turkish Cypriots) negative attitudes?

A third question explores the possible role of age. Is the internalization of national identity a linear function of age? In other words, do we expect to observe higher levels of the internalization of national identity in 11-year-olds compared to 7-year-olds? At a more theoretical level, does positive in-group bias decrease and positive out-group attitudes increase as cognitive developmental theory (Aboud, 1988; Aboud & Amato, 2001) suggests, or do children increase their negative out-group bias as they grow up as social identity development theory (SIDT; Nesdale 2004) claims?

METHOD

Participants

The participants of this study were 75 Greek-Cypriot children, 40 boys and 35 girls with mean age of 10.03 years. Eighteen children were classified in the

TABLE 1
Age by gender distribution of participants

Gender	7-years	11-years	Total
Males	10	30	40
Females	8	27	35
Total	18	57	75

group of 7-year-olds while 57 children comprised the 11-year-olds group (Table 1). Of the children, 81.3% ($n = 61$) were rated as not religious on a religiosity scale, while 18.7% ($n = 14$) were classified as moderately religious. All children were randomly selected from public schools of the Republic of Cyprus, they were all born in Cyprus, and they all had Greek-Cypriot parents. Prior to the selection process, the children were screened in terms of their socioeconomic background in order to represent the general socio-economic structure of Greek-Cypriot society.

Procedure

The children's National Identifications were assessed using the Strength of Identification Scale (SoIS; Barrett, 2007), while the children's national attitudes were assessed using a trait attribution task and affect questions. The participants were randomly selected from three elementary Greek-Cypriot schools in the district of Nicosia. All children were examined individually in a classroom especially provided by each school. Written consent was obtained from the parents of all the children that participated in our study. All measures were translated into Greek and then back translated into English by two research assistants. For full details of all the tasks and the procedures that were employed in their administration, see Barrett and Oppenheimer (2011 this issue). The target groups towards which the children's attitudes were assessed were Greek Cypriots (in-group), Turkish Cypriots (enemy out-group), Irish (neutral out-group 1) and Dutch (neutral out-group 2). In the present paper, only the data on attitudes to Greek Cypriots and Turkish Cypriots are reported.

RESULTS

Exploratory factor analysis

In order to examine whether the strength of National Identification manifests as a single construct in childhood, we computed an exploratory principal component analysis on the six items of the identification task.

TABLE 2
Psychometric properties of the national identification scale in the
Greek-Cypriot sample

Item	Factor loadings
Positive internalization of national identity	.72
Affect towards national identity	.70
Negative internalization of national identity	.68
Degree of national identity	.55
Pride of national identity	.44
Importance of national identity	.28

Note: Percentage of variance explained = 34.18; Cronbach alpha = .43.

The results for a single-factor solution show that in the Greek-Cypriot children the National Identification items do not load sufficiently on to a latent factor. The *KMO* index is at .60, which is considered relatively low despite the Bartlett's test of sphericity being statistically significant, $\chi^2(15) = 50.28$, $p < .001$. The loadings for the six items range from .28 to .72 for the six identification items and the percentage of variance explained is 34.18% (Table 2). Moreover, internal consistency analysis shows that the factor extracted from the solution is not reliable (Cronbach alpha = .43). Based on the above findings, we conclude that the National Identification Scale cannot be used as a unified construct and that further analysis requires that each item of that scale should be used independently from the other items.

Relationship between National Identification and in-group/out-group bias

In order to examine the relation between National Identification and in-group/out-group attitudes, we computed bivariate correlations (Pearson r) between the identification items and the total numbers of positive and negative adjectives assigned to each target group. Results show that none of the six identification items correlates significantly with either positive or negative attitudes towards the Turkish Cypriots. Pride for own nationality shows a significant positive correlation with positive in-group attitudes ($r = .28$, $p < .05$) and a significant negative correlation with negative in-group attitudes ($r = -.31$, $p < .01$). A significant negative correlation is also shown between the positive internalization of national identity and the negative in-group attitudes ($r = -.27$, $p < .05$).

As expected, the more the children express positive attitudes for their own national group the less negative attitudes they feel ($r = -.29$, $p < .05$). Further, the more positive attitudes they express for their in-group, the more they also express positive attitudes for the out-group ($r = .31$, $p < .01$).

In-group and out-group negative attitudes, however, do not correlate significantly ($r = -.03$, $p = .79$). Finally, positive and negative out-group attitudes are strongly negatively correlated ($r = -.66$, $p < .01$).

Based on the results of the correlation analysis, we proceeded to calculate the percentage of variance of in-group positive and out-group negative attitudes explained. Linear regression analysis confirms that none of the National Identification items predicts out-group negative attitudes. A large amount of variance, however, is predicted for out-group positive attitudes ($\beta = -0.65$, $p < .01$, $r^2 = .43$).

In-group positive attitudes are also not significantly predicted by national identification. Instead, they are significantly predicted by out-group positive attitudes ($\beta = 0.21$, $p < .05$) and negatively predicted by negative in-group attitudes ($\beta = -0.26$, $p < .01$). The two predictors account for 17% of the variance of the dependent measure.

Age and gender comparisons

A multivariate analysis of variance (MANOVA) was performed with all National Identification items and the in-group/out-group Attitudes as dependent measures and the Age and Gender as independent variables. Results show that younger children show significantly higher positive out-group Attitudes, $F(1, 62) = 9.25$, $p < .01$. The mean score for 7-year-olds were 2.71 ($SD = 2.26$) whereas for the 11-year-olds the mean score was 1.25 ($SD = 1.59$). Girls show significantly higher scores on the importance of the national identity, $F(1, 62) = 6.84$, $p < .05$. The girls' mean score was 4.39 ($SD = 1.18$) and for boys 3.90 ($SD = 1.25$). The importance of national identity also shows a significant interaction between Age and Gender, $F(1, 62) = 5.11$, $p < .05$. Younger girls show extremely higher scores (Mean $= 5.00$) than younger boys (Mean $= 3.20$), whereas older girls' (Mean $= 4.27$) and older boys' scores (Mean $= 4.14$) converge. This result, however, should be interpreted with caution since the younger girls' group consists of only eight participants, thus affecting the power of our analysis, and, additionally, the same group shows a ceiling effect since all girls in that group rated themselves at the highest score on the importance of national identity.

In-group vs. out-group attitudes

We further investigated whether in-group positive and negative attitudes are significantly higher than the respective out-group attitudes. Paired sample *t*-test shows that Greek-Cypriot children confirm the expected in-group favouritism hypothesis. In-group positive attitudes are significantly higher than out-group positive attitudes, $t(74) = 13.23$, $p < .01$, and out-group negative attitudes are significantly higher than in-group negative attitudes, $t(74) = 7.85$, $p < .01$. More interestingly, Greek-Cypriot children tend to assign more negative attributes towards the Turkish Cypriots than positive ones, $t(74) = 3.28$, $p < .01$. They also tend to evaluate neutral out-groups (i.e., the Irish and Dutch) less positively than the in-group, i.e., $t(74) = 4.86$, $p < .01$ and $t(74) = 4.94$, $p < .01$, respectively, while the neutral out-groups were evaluated significantly less negatively than the traditional enemy out-group (i.e., the Turkish Cypriots), $t(74) = 5.76$, $p < .01$ and $t(74) = 5.74$, $p < .01$, for the Irish and Dutch out-groups, respectively.

DISCUSSION

Our results are more in line with social identity development theory (Nesdale, 2004, 2008) and contrary to Aboud's CD approach (Aboud, 1988, 2008; Aboud & Amato, 2001; Doyle & Aboud, 1995; Doyle, Beaudet, & Aboud, 1988). Greek-Cypriot children are more positive toward the out-group (the traditional enemy) when they are younger. As they grow up they are less likely to perceive Turkish Cypriots in a positive manner. As SIDT suggests, context and socialization processes are influential factors during childhood that, especially in countries that have experienced conflict, are likely to prevent positive out-group perceptions from emerging. As previous researchers have claimed, education (e.g., Apple, 1993; Schleicher & Kozma, 1992) and especially formal schooling, which takes place between 6–12 years of age, operates as a mechanism that may change into a more negative manner the perceptions of children of groups labelled as enemies.

The relationship between National Identification and in-group/ out-group bias

As far as National Identification is concerned, despite previous findings and theories, our study does not confirm that the intensity of the internalization is related to in-group/out-group attitudes (e.g., social identity theory; Tajfel, 1978; Tajfel & Turner, 1986). Although we expected that the higher the identification the more the out-group negative attitudes, this was not confirmed. Instead, the only variable that predicted out-group negative attitudes was out-group positive attitudes; the more positively the children perceived the Turkish Cypriots, the less negative attitudes they had towards them.

National Identification does not appear to promote in-group positive attitudes as it did not promote negative out-group attitudes. These two findings run counter to our research hypotheses. What other factors could influence either out-group negative attitudes or in-group positive views that were not in the present study? Our study has confirmed a rather intuitive finding, namely that the more positively you see your enemy the less negative attitudes you tend to develop, and that when you see your enemy in a positive manner you also tend to see your own national group in a positive manner. In fact, in this case the traditional enemy ceases to be an enemy at all since children tend to assign positive attributes to the out-group.

The structure of National Identification

National Identification in Greek-Cypriot children does not appear to be a unified/single construct. Contrary to a widely held belief that during childhood a rather structured form of national identity is developed (e.g., Aboud & Doyle, 1993), our results show otherwise. Even though individual scores of the scale items are relatively high, they do not appear to correlate in such a way so that a latent factor would emerge. This result shows that Greek-Cypriot children by the age of 11 internalize to a great extent the various aspects of National Identification but they do not seem to bind together these aspects into a uniform psychological construct.

REFERENCES

Aboud, F. E. (1988). *Children and prejudice*. Oxford, UK: Blackwell.

Aboud, F. E. (2008). A social-cognitive developmental theory of prejudice. In S. M. Quintana & C. McKown (Eds.), *The handbook of race, racism and the developing child* (pp. 55–71). Hoboken, NJ: Wiley.

Aboud, F. E., & Amato, M. (2001). Developmental and socialization influences on intergroup bias. In R. Brown & S. L. Gaertner (Eds.), *Blackwell handbook of social psychology: Intergroup processes* (pp. 65–85). Oxford, UK: Blackwell.

Aboud, F. E., & Doyle, A. (1993). The early development of ethnic identity and attitudes. In M. Bernal & G. Knight (Eds.), *Ethnic identity: Formation and transmission among Hispanics and other minorities* (pp. 47–59). Albany, NY: State University of New York Press.

Apple, M. (1993). *Official knowledge: Democratic education in a conservative age*. London, UK: Routledge.

Barrett, M. (2007). *Children's knowledge, beliefs and feelings about nations and national groups*. Hove, UK: Psychology Press.

Barrett, M., & Oppenheimer, L. (2011). Findings, theories and methods in the study of children's national identifications and national attitudes. *European Journal of Developmental Psychology, 8*, 5–24.

Bar-Tal, D., & Teichman, Y. (2005). *Stereotypes and prejudice in conflict: Representations of Arabs in Israeli Jewish society*. Cambridge, UK: Cambridge University Press.

Bennett, M., Barrett, M., Karakozov, R., Kipiani, G., Lyons, E., Pavelnko, V., et al. (2004). Young children's evaluations of the ingroup and of outgroups: A multi-national study. *Social Development, 13*, 124–141.

Bennett, M., Lyons, E., Sani, F., & Barrett, M. (1998). Children's subjective identification with the group and ingroup favouritism. *Developmental Psychology, 34*, 902–909.

Bigler, R. S., Brown, C. S., & Markell, M. (2001). When groups are not created equal: Effects of group status on the formation of intergroup attitudes in children. *Child Development, 72*, 1151–1162.

Bigler, R. S., Jones, L. C., & Lobliner, D. B. (1997). Social categorization and the formation of intergroup attitudes in children. *Child Development, 66,* 1072–1087.

Doyle, A. B., & Aboud, F. E. (1995). A longitudinal study of White children's racial prejudice as a social-cognitive development. *Merrill-Palmer Quarterly, 41,* 209–228.

Doyle, A. B., Beaudet, J., & Aboud, F. E. (1988). Developmental patterns in the flexibility of children's ethnic attitudes. *Journal of Cross-Cultural Psychology, 19,* 3–18.

Mavratsas, C. (1998). *Facets of Greek nationalism in Cyprus: Ideological contest and the social construction of Greek-Cypriot identity 1974–1996.* Athens, Greece: Katarti.

Nesdale, D. (2004). Social identity processes and children's ethnic prejudice. In M. Bennett & F. Sani (Eds.), *The development of the social self* (pp. 219–245). Hove, UK: Psychology Press.

Nesdale, D. (2008). Social identity development and children's ethnic attitudes in Australia. In S. M. Quintana & C. McKown (Eds.), *The handbook of race, racism and the developing child* (pp. 313–338). Hoboken, NJ: Wiley.

Nesdale, D., & Flesser, D. (2001). Social identity and the development of children's group attitudes. *Child Development, 72*(2), 506–517.

Panteli, S. (1990). *The making of modern Cyprus: From obscurity to statehood.* Nicosia, Cyprus: Interwood Publications.

Papadakis, I. (1993). *Perceptions of history and collective identity: A study of contemporary Greek Cypriot and Turkish Cypriot nationalism.* Unpublished PhD thesis, University of Cambridge, UK.

Patrick, R. (1976). *Political geography and the Cyprus conflict, 1963–1971.* [Department of Geography Publications Series, 4]. Waterloo, Ontario: Faculty of Environmental Studies, University of Waterloo.

Poppe, E., & Linssen, H. (1999). Ingroup favouritism and the reflection of realistic dimensions of differences between national states in Central and Eastern European nationality stereotypes. *British Journal of Social Psychology, 38,* 85–102.

Portides, D., & Stavrinides, P. (2008). *Conflict and the construction of a common system of beliefs: The Cyprus paradigm.* Paper presented at the International Conference on Understanding Conflicts, Aarhus, Denmark, 19–22 August 2008.

Rutland, A. (1999). The development of national prejudice, in-group favouritism and self-stereotypes in British children. *British Journal of Social Psychology, 38,* 55–70.

Schleicher, K., & Kozma, T. (Eds.). (1992). *Ethnocentrism in education.* Frankfurt, Germany: Peter Lang.

Stavrinides, P. (2009). The psychological aspects of the Cyprus referendum. In H. Faustman & A. Varnava (Eds.), *The failure to reunify Cyprus: The Annan plan, the referendums of 2004 and the aftermath.* London, UK: I. B. Tauris.

Tajfel, H. (1978). Social categorization, social identity and social comparison. In H. Tajfel (Ed.), *Differentiation between social groups: Studies in the social psychology of intergroup relations* (pp. 61–76). London, UK: Academic Press.

Tajfel, H., & Turner, J. C. (1986). The social identity theory of intergroup behaviour. In S. Worchel & W. G. Austin (Eds.), *Psychology of intergroup relations* (2nd ed., pp. 7–24). Chicago, IL: Nelson-Hall.

Teichman, Y. (2001). The development of Israeli children's images of Jews and Arabs and their expression in human figure drawings. *Developmental Psychology, 37,* 749–776.

Teichman, Y., & Bar-Tal, D. (2008). Acquisition and development of a shared psychological intergroup repertoire in a context of intractable conflict. In S. M. Quintana & C. McKown (Eds.), *Handbook of race, racism, and the developing child* (pp. 452–482). New York, NY: Wiley.

EUROPEAN JOURNAL OF DEVELOPMENTAL PSYCHOLOGY
2011, 8 (1), 98–115

Ψ Psychology Press
Taylor & Francis Group

National identity and in-group/out-group attitudes with Basque and Basque-Spanish children growing up in the Basque Country

Luixa Reizábal and Garbiñe Ortiz

Faculty of Psychology, University of the Basque Country, Donostia (Gipuzkoa), Spain

National identity and in-group/out-group attitudes (evaluation and affect) as well as the relation of these variables to age, gender, and national group were investigated in 101 Basque children aged 7 and 11 years who belonged to the Basque and Basque-Spanish national groups. Findings show that the scores of the older Basque children on the six dimensions of National Identification were higher than those of Basque-Spanish children of the same age. For the 11-year-old Basque children, National Identification is more important than for their Basque-Spanish peers. With respect to in-group/out-group attitudes, both Basque and Basque-Spanish children show more positive attitudes (i.e., attributed more positive and less negative traits, and show higher positivity and likeability) towards their own in-group than towards the out-groups. The positive attitudes toward the in-group shown by the Basque children, however, are higher than those of the Basque-Spanish children. Moreover, Basque children's attitudes towards out-groups in general and towards the traditional enemy, in particular, are more negative than those of the Basque-Spanish children. Finally, while with Basque children certain dimensions of national identity correlated positively with positive attitudes toward the in-group and negatively with positive attitudes towards the traditional enemy, with Basque-Spanish children the same dimensions correlated positively with positive attitudes toward both the in-group and the national out-groups. Theoretical implications of these findings are discussed.

Keywords: Development; National identification; In-group/out-group attitudes; National group.

Correspondence should be addressed to Luixa Reizábal, Faculty of Psychology, University of the Basque Country, Tolosa Avenue 70, E-20018 Donostia (Gipuzkoa), Spain. E-mail: luixa.Reizábal@ehu.es

DOI: 10.1080/17405629.2010.534263

INTRODUCTION

This study investigated national identity and in-group/out-group attitudes as well as the relation of these variables to age, gender and the national group with children growing up in the Basque Country (Euskal Herria or Euskadi), one of the oldest nations in Europe. The Basque Country is located on the coast of the Bay of Biscay and has its own language, named Euskara, which is of pre-Indo-European origin and is spoken by over a quarter of the population. Presently, the Basque Country is a stateless nation divided over three political territories involving the Basque Autonomous Community involving the provinces of Alava, Biscay and Guipuzcoa and the Autonomous Community of Navarre in the Spanish State, as well as the ancient countries of Lower Navarre, Lapurdi and Zuberoa in the French Department of the Atlantic Pyrenees. This division has left the continental Basque Country in the north dependent on the French State, while the peninsular Basque Country, in turn, is dependent on the Spanish State.

In the Basque Country a strong nationalist movement is present, mainly in the peninsular part, where the present study was conducted. This movement has historical roots; some historians trace them back to the year AD 778, when Basques killed the rearguard of Charlemagne's army in the battle of Orreaga.

Numerous conflicts and wars took place prior to the nineteenth century because of annexing or centralizing rationales of kingdoms or states—mainly the Kingdoms of Castile and France. The latter states wished to incorporate the Basque provinces into their territory and to exercise sovereignty over the Basque people. Contemporary Basque nationalism emerged as a political movement at the end of the nineteenth and the beginning of the twentieth century. As a consequence of this nationalism, there has traditionally been a tendency to defend a different social reality or identity, one that includes a different language, a different culture, and different customs.

In 1936 the Spanish Civil War started, which had dramatic consequences for the peninsular Basque Country. On the one hand, thousands of Basques were killed by Franco's army and its allies such as the German Condor Legion, who bombed some Basque cities like Guernica. On the other hand, since 1939, when Franco won the Spanish Civil War, and during his Fascist dictatorship (1939–1975), all forms of self-government were violently suppressed, the use of the Basque language was banned, and various expressions of the Basque culture as well as Basque symbols were prohibited. In this situation, many Basque individuals became involved in the defence of the Basque Country's cultural and linguistic identity by different means, including political violence since 1958, the year in which ETA (Euskadi Ta Askatasuna, which means Basque Homeland and Freedom) was established.

Before his death, Franco stated that Juan Carlos I de Borbón would be his successor. When he died in 1975, the Transition process towards the Parliamentary Monarchy of Juan Carlos I began. A new Spanish Constitution was approved in December 1978 through a referendum by the majority of Spanish people, but only by 35% of the Basque voters. While this Constitution guarantees the right to autonomy for the nationalities and regions of the Spanish State, the "unity of Spain" is considered to be indivisible. As a consequence of this new Constitution, the peninsular part of the Basque Country was divided into the above mentioned two Autonomous Communities—the Basque Autonomous Community and the Autonomous Community of Navarre.

Nowadays, there is a strong social perception in the peninsular Basque Country of being different from the other parts of the Spanish State. However, this perception is not homogeneous for a number of reasons. One of the most important reasons is that the origin of a large proportion of the population of the Basque Country is formed by people who have immigrated from other parts of the Spanish State and from Castile and Extremadura, in particular. As a consequence, two competing visions with respect to the relationship between the Basque Country and the Spanish State are currently present within the peninsular part of the Basque Country. Whereas part of the population wants Spain to remain the only sovereign entity within the Basque territories, another part wants a new sovereignty status (i.e., an independent Basque State) or at least the right of the Basque Country to decide its own future (i.e., the right of self-determination).

With this political history and context in mind, the present study focused in particular upon the relationship between children's age, gender, and national group, and the evaluative and affective attitudes that they exhibited towards their national in-group and selected national out-groups. The Basque Country provides a particularly interesting context in which to explore these issues. This is because national identity is constructed in very different ways by different individuals living in this country. Research with adults has revealed that three different national identities can be developed in the Basque Country. These identities are characterized by: (i) people who exhibit a strong positive identification with the Basque national group and do not identify with the Spanish national group (i.e., National identity); (ii) people who exhibit an absence of identification with the Basque national group and a strong positive identification with the Spanish national group (i.e., State identity); and finally (iii) people who show a strong identification with both the Spanish and the Basque national groups (i.e., National-State identity; Reizábal, 1995).

Moreover, previous research has shown that there is a relationship between national identity and the conceptualization of peace, and when national identity is made salient, there is a relationship between national identity and attitudes towards out-groups (Reizábal, 1995). In relation to children's in-group and out-group attitudes, previous research in the Basque Country has demonstrated that both National Identification and evaluations of, and feelings towards national in-groups and out-groups are associated with the language(s) spoken in the family home (Reizábal, Valencia, & Barrett, 2004).

METHOD

Participants

Several primary schools of the Basque Country were invited to participate in the research by means of a personal contact with their directors. Unfortunately, the majority of them rejected the invitation arguing that the research was of "political content". Thus, only two of the invited schools accepted participation in the study. In these schools 118 children (59 male and 59 female) aged 7 (range: 7 years to 7 years and 11 months) and 11 (range: 11 years to 11 years and 11 months) years old living in the Basque Country were interviewed. Depending upon the responses to questions dealing with the child's degree of Basque and Spanish identifications, participants were categorized into the following national groups: (i) a Spanish group, consisting of children who described themselves as "*very Spanish*", "*quite Spanish*" or "*little bit Spanish*" and "*not at all Basque*" ($n = 6$); (ii) a Basque group, consisting of children who described themselves as "*very Basque*", "*quite Basque*" or "*little bit Basque*" and "*not at all Spanish*" ($n = 46$, 31 boys and 15 girls); and (iii) a Basque-Spanish group, which consisted of children who described themselves as "*very Spanish*" or "*quite Spanish*" or "*little bit Spanish*" and "*very Basque*" or "*quite Basque*" or "*little bit Basque*" ($n = 55$, 25 boys and 30 girls). Because only 6 children were categorized in the Spanish group, it was decided to omit them from the sample, as well as the children who answered "don't know" to these questions. Thus, finally 46 Basque children with mean ages 7.05 ($n = 17$) and 11.05 ($n = 29$) and 55 Basque-Spanish children with mean ages 7.06 ($n = 28$) and 11.06 ($n = 27$) participated in this study (information about the number of girls and boys in each national group is shown in Table 1). Parental permission was obtained for the children's participation in the study.

Materials

In this study, the common measures and procedure described by Barrett and Oppenheimer (2011 this issue) were used, although the following changes were introduced:

TABLE 1

Mean scores (and standard deviations) for the six dimensions of the National Identity Scale for the two national groups, age groups, and gender

| | Basque children | | | | | | | Basque-Spanish children | | | | | | |
| | 7 | | | 11 | | | All | 7 | | | 11 | | | All |
NI-aspects	Boy (n=10)	Girl (n=6)	Total (n=16)	Boy (n=18)	Girl (n=9)	Total (n=27)	Total (n=43)	Boy (n=12)	Girl (n=11)	Total (n=23)	Boy (n=8)	Girl (n=15)	Total (n=23)	Total (n=46)
Degree	4.63 (0.63)	4.55 (0.69)	4.61 (0.63)	4.73 (0.69)	4.85 (0.47)	4.77 (0.63)	4.71 (0.62)	3.95 (0.63)	3.90 (0.81)	3.93 (0.71)	3.60 (0.47)	3.37 (0.64)	3.47 (0.58)	3.70 (0.68)
Affect	4.91 (0.31)	5.00 (0.00)	4.93 (0.25)	4.83 (0.38)	4.89 (0.33)	4.85 (0.36)	4.88 (0.32)	4.37 (0.71)	4.54 (0.57)	4.45 (0.64)	3.87 (0.69)	3.80 (0.45)	3.82 (0.53)	4.14 (0.66)
PosInt	4.90 (0.31)	5.00 (0.00)	4.94 (0.25)	4.89 (0.32)	4.78 (0.66)	4.85 (0.45)	4.88 (0.39)	4.50 (1.14)	4.59 (0.49)	4.54 (0.87)	4.50 (0.53)	4.10 (0.60)	4.23 (0.60)	4.39 (0.76)
NegInt	4.30 (0.82)	4.83 (0.41)	4.50 (0.73)	4.55 (0.70)	4.44 (0.88)	4.52 (0.75)	4.51 (0.73)	4.37 (0.61)	4.40 (0.43)	4.39 (0.52)	3.93 (0.56)	3.66 (0.55)	3.76 (0.56)	4.07 (0.62)
Importance	4.37 (0.66)	4.58 (0.64)	4.45 (0.64)	4.86 (0.40)	4.72 (0.55)	4.81 (0.45)	4.68 (0.55)	4.06 (0.68)	4.03 (0.85)	4.04 (0.75)	3.82 (1.31)	3.50 (0.84)	3.61 (1.01)	3.83 (0.91)
Pride	3.87 (1.37)	4.16 (1.51)	3.98 (1.38)	4.72 (0.53)	4.72 (0.55)	4.72 (0.53)	4.44 (0.99)	4.32 (0.49)	4.48 (0.61)	4.40 (0.55)	4.14 (0.57)	3.70 (0.72)	3.85 (0.69)	4.13 (0.68)

Note: PosInt = Positive Internalization; NegInt = Negative Internalization.

Strength of Identification Scale (SoIS; Barrett, 2007). Due to the fact that in the Basque Country there are two different national groups with which children can identify (i.e., Basque and Spanish), the possibility of identifying with either or both the Basque and Spanish national groups was included in the six items of the SoIS. As explained in the participants section, children were categorized as falling into the Basque or the Basque-Spanish group depending upon the responses to questions dealing with the degree of Basque and Spanish identifications. In this way, in the other five items of the SoIS, participants categorized into the Basque group were asked about Basque identification, while children categorized into the Basque-Spanish group were asked about both Basque and Spanish identifications.

In-group/out-group attitudes. The attitudes towards the following five national groups were analysed: (i) Basque (i.e., in-group); (ii) Spanish (i.e., the in-group for the Basque-Spanish group and the traditional enemy 1 for the Basque group—see the introduction); (iii) French (i.e., the traditional enemy 2 for the Basque group—see the introduction—and the traditional enemy 1 for the Basque-Spanish group, because Spain has had different armed conflicts with this country in its history, such as the Spanish War of Independence of 1808); (iv) English (i.e., the traditional enemy 2 for Basque-Spanish group, due to the fact that Spain had several armed conflicts such as the Anglo-Spanish War between 1796 and 1808); and (v) Italian (i.e., the neutral out-group for both groups).

Four separate translators translated the interview and response cards independently from English into Euskara and Spanish. The four translations were compared, and any discrepancies resolved by discussion. The agreed-upon translation was then translated back again into English by a fifth independent translator and compared with the original English instrument in order to ensure that no alterations in meaning had occurred as a result of the translation process. Due to fact that Spanish has feminine and masculine adjective suffixes, three versions of the interview and sets of response cards were prepared, two in Spanish (i.e., one in each gender) and one in Euskara.

Procedure

Each child was interviewed individually in a quiet room made available in their school. After establishing rapport with the child, it was explained that the interviewer was interested in finding out what the child thought about certain things. Reassurance was given that this was not a test, that there were no right or wrong answers, and that their answers would be treated anonymously. Children were asked to report their age and gender.

Only one version of the interview and set of response cards was used with each individual child, depending on the language the child spontaneously spoke to the interviewer at their initial meeting (Euskara or Spanish) and gender (i.e., male or female if the child spoke Spanish). For full details of all the tasks and the procedures that were employed in their administration, see Barrett and Oppenheimer (2011 this issue).

RESULTS

Strength of Identification Scale (SoIS)

A principal component analysis with varimax rotation on the six National Identification scores resulted in a two-factor model with the Basque participants. Both factors explained 57.13% of variance and showed importance, degree, pride, and affect to load on the first factor and positive and negative internalization on the second. Because the Basque-Spanish participants had two scores on each dimension, relating to the Basque and Spanish identifications respectively, the mean scores on each dimension were calculated in order to obtain an estimate of the child's overall level of National Identification, and the principal component analysis was then conducted on these mean scores. This analysis revealed a two-factor model explaining 64.13% of the variance. The mean scores of importance, degree, pride and negative internalization loaded on the first factor and mean scores of affect and positive internalization on the second.

When a one-factor model for the data of the Basque and Basque-Spanish children was requested, the obtained two structural models showed different loadings and relations between dimensions of identification for each group (see Figures 1A and 1B).

Based on these findings, it appeared more sensible to treat the aspects of National Identification as separate variables and to examine the interrelations among in-group/out-group attitudes and the aspects of National Identification separately for each national group. Consequently, first the analyses of the SoIS are presented for the Basque and Basque-Spanish participants separately followed by comparative analyses.

National Identity Scale

The Basque group. A 2 × 2 (Age × Gender) multivariate analysis of variance (MANOVA) on the six dimensions of the SoIS (see Table 1) revealed a significant main effect of Age for pride only, $F(1, 41) = 5.34$, $p < .05$, showing that with Basque children pride in their National Identification (i.e., 3.98 vs. 4.72 with the 7- and 11-year-olds, respectively)

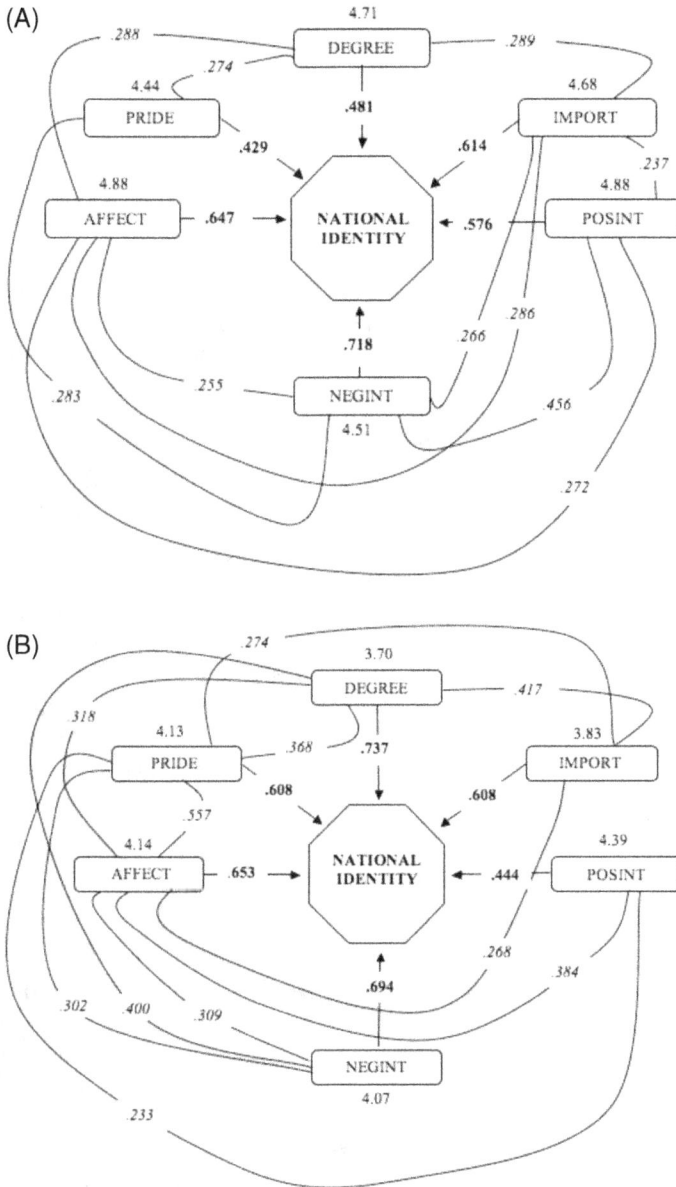

Figure 1. A schematic representation of the one-factor structure of National Identification, showing the factor loadings for (**bold**), the mean scores of, and the correlations (*italics, p < .05*) among the dimensions of National Identification for the Basque (A) and Basque-Spanish children (B).

increases across age. No significant effects were found for Gender or the Age by Gender interaction.

The Basque-Spanish group. Similarly, a MANOVA was conducted on the mean scores of the six SoIS dimension with the Basque-Spanish children. Also with the Basque-Spanish participants no significant effects were present for the Age by Gender interaction or for Gender. Four significant effects for Age were present concerning degree, $F(1, 51) = 6.03$, $p < .05$, affect, $F(1, 51) = 18.01$, $p < .001$, negative internalization, $F(1, 51) = 16.27$, $p < .001$, and pride, $F(1, 51) = 7.89$, $p < .01$. These findings show that with Basque-Spanish children degree of National Identification (i.e., 3.93 vs. 3.47, with the 7- and 11-year-olds, respectively), affect towards National Identification (i.e., 4.45 vs. 3.82), and national pride (i.e., 4.40 vs. 3.85) decrease across age and that when others evaluate the Basque and the Spanish groups negatively, Basque-Spanish children at age 11 experienced less negative feelings than at age 7 (i.e., 3.76 vs. 4.39).

The Basque vs. the Basque-Spanish group. A $2 \times 2 \times 2$ (National Group $\times$ Age $\times$ Gender) MANOVA on the six dimensions of the SoIS did not reveal any significant effect for the three-way interaction (i.e., National Group by Age by Gender), nor for the two-way interactions between Age and Gender and between Nation and Gender. The interaction between National Group and Age showed significant effects for degree, $F(1, 93) = 5.38$, $p < .05$, affect, $F(1, 93) = 8.16$, $p < .01$, importance, $F(1, 93) = 4.24$, $p < .05$, and for pride, $F(1, 93) = 12.83$, $p = .001$. With the exception of pride, for all other dimensions of the SoIS significant main effects for National Group were present, i.e., with $F(1, 93)$-values being 51.66, 52.12, 11.12, 14.26, and 15.62 and $p < .001$ for degree, affect, negative and positive internalization, and importance, respectively.

Post hoc analyses showed that the interaction for the degree of identification confirmed the earlier reported effect of age in the Basque-Spanish group; moreover, 7- and 11-year-old Basque children showed a higher degree of identification (i.e., 4.61 vs. 3.77, respectively) than 7- and 11-year-old Basque-Spanish children (i.e., 3.93 vs. 3.47, respectively). In relation to the dimension of affect, post hoc analyses confirmed the influence of age in the Basque-Spanish group and showed that 7- and 11-year-old Basque children (i.e., 4.93 vs. 4.85) showed higher affect than 7- and 11-year-old Basque-Spanish children (i.e., 4.45 vs. 3.82).

In relation to importance and pride, post hoc analyses showed that 11-year-old Basque children attributed higher importance to National Identification and felt more proud than 11-year-old Basque-Spanish children (i.e., 4.81 vs. 3.61 for importance, and 4.72 vs. 3.85 for pride).

As was noted before, with the exception of pride with their National Identification, the Basque children showed significant higher levels for degree (i.e., 4.71 vs. 3.70), affect (i.e., 4.88 vs. 4.14), positive (i.e., 4.88 vs.4.39) and negative internalization (i.e., 4.51 vs. 4.07), and importance (i.e., 4.68 vs. 3.83) than their Basque-Spanish peers.

In sum, the results about National Identification showed that age had different influences within each of the two national groups and that the groups differed in National Identification (i.e., for five out of the six dimensions of National Identification the Basque children demonstrated higher levels than the Basque-Spanish children).

In-group/out-group attitudes

The Basque group. Analyses were conducted on: (i) the mean numbers of *positive and negative traits* assigned to the in-group (Basque people), two traditional enemy out-groups (traditional enemy 1 = Spain; traditional enemy 2 = France), and a neutral out-group (Italy); (ii) the difference scores based on the deduction of the negative from the positive traits for each group (i.e., *positivity*); and (iii) feelings towards each group (i.e., *liking*). The mean scores are shown in Table 2.

Positive and negative traits assigned to each group. Separate MANOVAs were run on the number of positive and negative traits assigned to each group. In the first MANOVA, Age was used as independent variable. This analysis showed three significant effects of Age with respect to positive traits for the traditional enemy 1, $F(1, 42) = 11.54$, $p < .01$, the traditional enemy 2, $F(1, 42) = 4.32$, $p < .05$, and the neutral out-group, $F(1, 42) = 7.07$, $p < .05$.

These findings suggest that Basque children at age 11 attributed less positive traits to the traditional enemy 1 (i.e., Spain), the traditional enemy 2 (i.e., France) and the neutral out-group (i.e., Italy) than at age 7 (i.e., .76 vs. 2.40 for traditional enemy 1; 2.14 vs. 3.27 for traditional enemy 2; 2.17 vs. 3.73 for the neutral out-group). In the second MANOVA Gender was used as independent variable. No significant effects involving Gender were found.

Positivity. Separate MANOVAs were run on the overall positivity scores. In the first MANOVA, Age was used as the independent variable. Two significant effects of Age were evident with respect to positivity towards the traditional enemy 1, $F(1, 42) = 5.28$, $p < .05$, and the neutral out-group, $F(1, 42) = 5.9$, $p < .05$, suggesting that Basque children at age 11 show significantly less positivity towards the traditional enemy 1 (i.e., Spain) and the neutral out-group (i.e., Italy) than at age 7 (i.e., -1.72 vs. -0.33 for the traditional enemy 1 and $+1.17$ vs. $+2.86$ for the neutral out-group,

TABLE 2
The mean number of positive and negative trait attributions to, positivity and likeability
ratings of the in-group and two out-groups by Basque and Basque-Spanish children

	Traits			
	Pos.	*Neg.*	*Pos. – Neg.*	*Liking*
Basque children				
In-group: Basque	4.27	0.45	+3.81	4.90
Enemy out-group 1: Spain	1.32	2.34	– 1.02	2.05
Enemy out-group 2: France	2.52	1.25	+1.27	3.10
Neutral out-group: Italy	2.70	0.95	+1.75	3.27
Basque-Spanish children				
In-group: Basque & Spain	3.37	0.66	+2.71	4.29
Enemy out-group 1: France	2.94	1.00	1.94	3.37
Enemy out-group 2: England	3.08	0.70	+2.37	3.85
Neutral out-group: Italy	2.96	0.79	+2.16	3.29

Note: Pos. – Neg. = Positivity (deduction of negative from positive traits).

respectively). Moreover, separate paired t-tests revealed that the in-group was evaluated significantly more positively than out-groups, $t(45) = 8.72$, $p < .001$, $t(43) = 6.72$, $p < .001$ and $t(43) = 5.05$, $p < .001$, for traditional enemy 1, enemy 2 and neutral out-group, respectively, while the traditional enemy 1 was also evaluated less positively than the traditional enemy 2 and neutral out-group, $t(43) = -4.72$, $p < .001$ and $t(43) = -5.96$, $p < .001$, respectively. However, the traditional enemy 2 and neutral out-group were similarly evaluated. In the second MANOVA, Gender was used as the independent variable. No significant effects involving Gender were found in this analysis.

Feelings towards each group. With respect to feelings (i.e., liking) towards the in-group and out-groups, separate MANOVAs were run. In the first one, Age was used as the independent variable and in the second one, Gender. No significant effects of these variables were found. However, separate paired t-tests revealed that the liking for the in-group was higher than liking for the out-groups, $t(43) = 12.32$, $p < .001$, $t(42) = 9.72$, $p < .001$ and $t(41) = 7.30$, $p < .001$, for traditional enemy 1, enemy 2 and neutral out-group, respectively, while the traditional enemy 1 was liked less than the traditional enemy 2 and the neutral out-group, $t(42) = -.87$, $p < .001$ and $t(43) = -5.23$, $p < .001$, respectively, and no significant difference was found between feelings toward the traditional enemy 2 and the neutral out-group.

The Basque-Spanish group. The MANOVA analyses run on the number of positive and negative traits, on positivity and on feelings towards the Basque and the Spanish in-groups, French and English traditional enemies and Italian neutral out-group did not reveal any significant effect for Age nor for Gender. Separate paired t-tests were run to account for differences between evaluations about in-group and out-groups. These results showed only one difference on evaluation about groups, namely, the in-group was evaluated significantly more positively than the traditional enemy 1, $t(52) = 2.72$, $p < .01$. However, in relation to feelings, likeability scores of the in-group were higher than those of out-groups, $t(51) = 4.59$, $p < .001$, $t(52) = 2.50$, $p < .05$ and $t(52) = 5.28$, $p < .001$, for traditional enemy 1, enemy 2 and neutral out-group, respectively, and the likeability score of the traditional enemy 2 was higher than that attributed to the neutral out-group, $t(54) = 2.59$, $p < .05$.

The Basque vs. the Basque-Spanish group

Positive and negative traits assigned to each group. Separate MANOVAs were run. The first analysis run was a 2×2 (National Group $\times$ Age) MANOVA. An interaction effect was found on the number of positive adjectives attributed to the traditional enemy 1, $F(1, 93) = 4.14$, $p < .05$. Post hoc analyses confirmed the influence of Age found in the Basque group and showed that 11-year-old Basque-Spanish children attributed more positive adjectives to the traditional enemy 1 than 11-year-old Basque children (i.e., 2.78 vs. 0.76). Results also showed main effects of National Group on the number of positive adjectives attributed to the in-group, $F(1, 93) = 10.53$, $p < .01$, to the traditional enemy 1, $F(1, 93) = 18.21$, $p < .001$, as well as in the number of negative adjectives attributed to the traditional enemy 1, $F(1, 93) = 14.58$, $p < .001$, and to the traditional enemy 2, $F(1, 93) = 4.65$, $p < .05$. These results showed that Basque children attributed more positive adjectives to the in-group (4.27 vs. 3.37), less positive adjectives to the traditional enemy 1 (1.32 vs. 2.94) and more negative adjectives to the traditional enemy 1 (2.34 vs. 1.00) and to the traditional enemy 2 (1.25 vs. 0.70) than Basque-Spanish children. In relation to Age, main effects were found for the number of positive adjectives attributed to the traditional enemy 2, $F(1, 93) = 6.31$, $p < .05$, and to the neutral out-group, $F(1, 93) = 9.06$, $p < .01$, showing that 7-year-old children attribute more positive adjectives to the traditional enemy 2 (i.e., 3.34 vs. 2.45) and to the neutral out-group (i.e., 3.41 vs. 2.43) than 11-year-olds.

The second analysis conducted was a 2×2 (National Group $\times$ Gender) MANOVA. No significant effects involving Gender were found, although results confirmed the main effects of National Group found in the previous MANOVA.

Positivity.   Separate MANOVA analyses were run. The first one was a 2×2 (National Group $\times$ Gender) MANOVA. No interaction effect was found, although main effects of National Group were found on positivity towards the in-group, $F(1, 93) = 11.26$, $p < .001$, the traditional enemy 1, $F(1, 93) = 27.98$, $p = .001$, and the traditional enemy 2, $F(1, 93) = 4.08$, $p < .05$. These results indicate that Basque children show higher positivity towards the in-group ($+3.81$ vs. $+2.71$) and lower towards to the traditional enemy 1 (-1.02 vs. $+1.94$), and enemy 2 ($+1.27$ vs. $+2.37$) than Basque-Spanish children. No significant main effect of Gender was found.

The second analysis run was a 2×2 (National Group $\times$ Age) MANOVA. No interaction effect was found, while the main effects of National Group on positivity towards the above mentioned groups were confirmed. In relation to Age, main effects were found for positivity towards the traditional enemy 1, $F(1, 93) = 8.01$, $p < .01$, and the neutral out-group, $F(1, 93) = 8.82$, $p < .01$. Post hoc analyses indicated that 11-year-old children show lower positivity toward the traditional enemy 1 (-0.16 vs. $+1.63$, respectively) and the neutral out-group (1.46 vs. 2.68, respectively) than 7-year-olds.

Feelings towards each group.   Separate MANOVAs on the likeability scores for each group were run. The first 2×2 (National Group $\times$ Gender) MANOVA revealed only a trend interaction effect for the likeability score attributed to the neutral out-group, $F(1, 89) = 3.85$, $p = .053$, showing that Basque boys attribute higher likeability score to the neutral out-group than Basque girls (i.e., 3.48 vs. 2.86), while Basque-Spanish boys attribute lower likeability score to the neutral out-group than Basque-Spanish girls (i.e., 3.00 vs. 3.54). Results also show main effects for National Group on the likeability scores attributed to the in-group, $F(1, 89) = 29.13$, $p < .001$, to the traditional enemy 1, $F(1, 89) = 20.66$, $p < .001$, and enemy 2, $F(1, 89) = 7.94$, $p < .01$. Post hoc analyses revealed that Basque children showed higher likeability toward the in-group and lower likeability toward the traditional enemy 1 and traditional enemy 2 than Basque-Spanish children (4.90 vs.4.29, respectively, for the in-group; 2.05 vs.3.37, respectively, for the traditional enemy 1; and 3.10 vs.3.85, respectively, for the traditional enemy 2). No significant main effect of Gender was found.

The second 2×2 (National Group $\times$ Age) MANOVA revealed an interaction effect for the likeability score attributed to the in-group, $F(1, 89) = 3.49$, $p = .065$. Post hoc analyses showed that this effect was due to the fact that 11-year-old Basque children attribute higher likeability score to the in-group than 11-year-old Basque-Spanish children (i.e., 4.90 and 4.29, respectively). The main effects of National Group for likeability scores attributed to the in-group, to the traditional enemy 1 and the traditional enemy 2 in the 2×2 (National Group $\times$ Gender) MANOVA were confirmed.

In relation to Age, a trend main effect was present for the likeability scores of the traditional enemy 1, $F(1, 89) = 3.38$, $p = .069$. Post hoc analyses showed that 7-year-old children attributed higher likeability scores to the traditional enemy 1 than 11-year-old children (i.e., 3.17 vs. 2.47).

It should be noted that, although we were conscious of statistical limitations, a MANOVA analysis was run with all independent variables of the design (i.e., National Group, Age Group and Gender). This analysis confirmed results described in this section and show a Gender by Age interaction effect on the number of negative adjectives attributed to the in-group, $F(1, 89) = 4.10$, $p < .05$, and on liking towards the in-group, $F(1, 85) = 8.62$, $p < .01$. In relation to the number of negative adjectives attributed to the in-group, results show that 7-year-old boys attributed more negative adjectives to the in-group than girls of the same age (i.e., 0.92 vs. 0.40) and that 11-year-old boys attributed fewer negative adjectives to the in-group than girls of the same age (i.e., 0.34 vs. 0.64), but post hoc analysis did not confirm this difference.

In relation to liking scores towards the in-group, results show that 7-year-old girls showed higher likeability scores towards the in-group than boys of the same age (i.e., 4.57 vs. 4.38) and that 11-year-old boys showed higher likeability scores towards the in-group than girls of the same age (4.76 vs. 4.37), although post hoc analysis did not confirm these differences.

In sum, results showed that the national groups were different with respect to in-group/out-group attitudes, and that age influenced these attitudes. On the one hand, Basque children showed more positive attitudes and feelings toward the in-group and more negative attitudes and feelings toward the traditional enemies than Basque-Spanish children. On the other hand, younger children had more positive attitudes towards out-groups than older children.

National Identification and in-group/out-group attitudes

The final part of the analyses involved the examination of relationships between dimensions of National Identification and measures used to analyse in-group/out-group attitudes (i.e., the number of positive and negative traits attributed to each group, positivity and likeability). The relationship between these variables was analysed for each national group separately. Out of a total of 36 correlation coefficients with each group, four significant correlations were found with the Basque group. These involved the relationship between degree of identification and positive traits attributed to and positivity towards the traditional enemy 1 (i.e., Spain), $r(46) = -.30$, $p < .05$ and $r(46) = -.31$, $p < .05$, respectively; between negative internalization and negative traits attributed to the in-group, $r(46) = -.30$, $p < .01$, positivity towards and likeability of the traditional enemy 2 (i.e.,

France), $r(46) = .30$, $p < .05$ and $r(46) = .37$, $p < .05$, respectively; and between pride and negative traits attributed to and positivity towards the in-group, $r(46) = -.47$, $p < .01$ and $r(46) = .37$, $p < .05$, respectively.

With respect to the Basque-Spanish children, correlations were found between degree and likeability of the in-group, $r(55) = .31$, $p < .05$; between affect and likeability of the in-group and of the traditional enemy 1 (i.e., France), $r(55) = .52$, $p < .01$ and $r(55) = .28$, $p < .05$, respectively; between importance and positive traits attributed to the in-group, $r(55) = .35$, $p < .01$, to the traditional enemy 1, $r(55) = .30$, $p < .05$, and the neutral out-group ($r = .46$, $p < .01$), as well as the positivity towards the in-group, $r(55) = .35$, $p < .05$, and the neutral out-group, $r(55) = .48$, $p < .01$; and finally, between pride and positive traits attributed to, $r(55) = .31$, $p < .05$, positivity, $r(55) = .40$, $p < .01$, and likeability towards the in-group, $r(55) = .44$, $p < .01$.

DISCUSSION

The purpose of this study was to examine national identity and in-group/out-group attitudes (evaluations and feelings) with children aged 7 and 11 who are raised in the Basque Country. These variables were examined in terms of their relationship with one another and in terms of their development and the level to which they are influenced by age, gender and national group membership.

In accordance with earlier findings with Basque adults (Reizábal, 1995), children living in the Basque Country develop three different national identities involving: (i) a strong positive identification with the Basque group and an absence of identification with the Spanish group (National identity); or (ii) an absence of identification with the Basque group and a strong positive identification with the Spanish group (State identity); or (iii) a strong identification with both the Spanish and the Basque groups (National-State identity).

In relation to National Identification and contrary to earlier findings with children from a range of national and ethnic groups (Barrett 2007; see Barrett & Oppenheimer, 2011 this issue), the six dimensions of National Identification did not form a unitary construct with either national group but related in different constellations to National Identification for both groups. Thus, the SoIS falls apart in the Basque Country, presumably because national identities are more complex and children have more nuanced understandings of their national identities in this country than in other locations. The absence of a unitary construct of National Identification demanded the separate examination of each dimension. It was found that Basque children score higher than Basque-Spanish children on five of the six dimensions of National Identification, implying that one's belonging to the Basque national group plays an important role in the Basque Country. Whereas 7-year-old Basque children score higher in all dimensions except pride than Basque-Spanish children at that age, 11-year-old Basque children score higher on the six dimensions of the SoIS. Moreover, while degree, affect, positive internalization, negative internalization, importance and pride decrease with age with Basque-Spanish children, such reductions were not observed with Basque children, probably because national identity is more salient for these children. No effect of gender upon National Identification was found.

There was evidence of in-group bias, whereby both Basque and Basque-Spanish children showed more positive and less negative attitudes (evaluations and feelings) towards their own in-group than the out-groups. Moreover, in-group bias shown by Basque children was higher than that of the Basque-Spanish children. Basque children's attitudes towards out-groups in general and traditional enemies in particular are more negative than those of the Basque-Spanish children, probably due to Basque people's perception that they live in a country in political conflict and in which clear "enemies" are present (mainly Spain but also France). These findings confirm a social identity theory (SIT) prediction (Tajfel & Turner, 1986), which states that children with stronger National Identification will rate their in-group more highly than out-groups. Moreover, it could be that the Basque group perceives the political situation as illegitimate and changeable, something that would not be perceived in the same way by the Basque-Spanish group (Rubin & Hewstone, 2004).

Finally, with Basque children some dimensions of National Identification (i.e., degree, negative internalization and pride) are related to more positive attitudes towards the in-group and more negative attitudes toward the traditional enemy 1 (i.e., Spain). As we noted earlier, this finding might be due to the perception of Basque people that they live in a country in political conflict and in which clear "enemies" are present (i.e., primarily Spain). These findings confirm the above mentioned SIT prediction (Tajfel & Turner, 1986). However, with Basque-Spanish children some dimensions of National Identification (i.e., degree, affect, importance and pride) are related to *both* positive attitudes toward the in-group and the national out-groups, a finding that raises problems for the above-mentioned prediction from social identity theory.

While in-group/out-group attitudes with Basque-Spanish children were not affected by age, the number of positive traits attributed to and the positivity towards the national out-groups decrease with age with Basque children. This is probably due to the fact that these children are developing in the context of an "intractable conflict" (Teichman & Bar-Tal, 2008, p. 453) in which a greater awareness of threat, salience of the differences between groups and the intensification of national identity can occur

(Teichman & Bar-Tal, 2008). These findings raise problems for cognitive-developmental theory (CDT) of the development of intergroup attitudes (Aboud, 1988; Doyle & Aboud, 1995; Doyle, Beaudet, & Aboud, 1988). CDT predicts that there should be a reduction of in-group bias between the ages of 6 and 12, irrespective of the specific national context in which children are growing up.

In sum, the findings of the present study do not fully support the predictions made by SIDT, CDT and SIT. As a consequence, we believe that the present findings are better explained by societal-social-cognitive-motivational theory (SSCMT), which postulates that development in driven by *national enculturation* processes through which children acquire a subjective sense of personal affiliation and belonging to their own nation and/or state (Barrett, 2007). Thus, it could be argued that in the context of the Basque Country at the beginning of the twenty-first century, children participate in cultural traditions, practices and customs of their own nation and/or state and identify subjectively with their own nation (i.e., Basque identity), State (i.e., Spanish identity) or both (i.e., Basque-Spanish identity). Keeping in mind that each national identity consists of a complex structure of knowledge, beliefs and feelings concerning the national in-group and relevant comparison out-groups (Barrett, 2007), differences between Basque and Basque-Spanish children's structure and level of National Identification as well as in-group/out-group attitudes would be related to the fact of belonging of different national groups.

Although many significant findings and trends in the data have been discussed there are a number of limitations to the present study. The sample size was relatively small, consisting of 101 children (i.e., 46 children assigned to the Basque and 55 to the Basque-Spanish group). In addition, the limited age range studied (i.e., 7- and 11-year-olds) may have obscured additional changes across age. Both limitations may considerably reduce the general-izability of the present findings. In future research larger numbers of participants should be included in each national and gender group and the age range should be expanded.

REFERENCES

Aboud, F. E. (1988). *Children and prejudice*. Oxford, UK: Blackwell.

Barrett, M. (2007). *Children's knowledge, beliefs and feelings about nations and national groups.* Hove, UK: Psychology Press.

Barrett, M., & Oppenheimer, L. (2011). Findings, theories and methods in the study of children's national identifications and national attitudes. *European Journal of Developmental Psychology, 8,* 5–24.

Doyle, A. B., & Aboud, F. E. (1995). A longitudinal study of White children's racial prejudice as a social-cognitive development. *Merrill-Palmer Quarterly, 41,* 209–228.

Doyle, A. B., Beaudet, J., & Aboud, F. E. (1988). Developmental patterns in the flexibility of children's ethnic attitudes. *Journal of Cross-Cultural Psychology, 19*, 3–18.

Reizábal, L. (1995). *Bakearen dimentsio kulturala Euskal Herriko Uste Sistema eta Pertzepzioetan [Cultural dimension of peace in belief-systems and perceptions of the Basque Country].* Bilbao, Spain: UPV/EHU.

Reizábal, L., Valencia, J., & Barrett, M. (2004). National identifications and attitudes to national ingroups and outgroups among children living in the Basque Country. *Infant and Child Development, 13*, 1–20.

Rubin, M., & Hewstone, M. (2004). Social identity, system justification and social dominance: Commentary on Reicher, Jost et al., and Sidanius et al. *Political Psychology, 25*, 823–844.

Tajfel, H., & Turner, J. C. (1986). The social identity theory of intergroup behaviour. In S. Worchel & W. G. Austin (Eds.), *Psychology of intergroup relations.* (pp. 7–24). Chicago, IL: Nelson-Hall.

Teichman, Y., & Bar-Tal, D. (2008). Acquisition and development of a shared psychological intergroup repertoire in a context of intractable conflict. In S. M. Quintana & C. McKown (Eds.), *Handbook of race, racism, and the developing child.* (pp. 452–482). New York, NY: Wiley.

EUROPEAN JOURNAL OF DEVELOPMENTAL PSYCHOLOGY
2011, 8 (1), 116–132

Ψ Psychology Press
Taylor & Francis Group

Comparative analyses: Are there discernable patterns in the development of and relationships among National Identification and in-group/out-group attitudes?

Louis Oppenheimer

Department of Psychology, University of Amsterdam, Amsterdam, The Netherlands

The purpose of this concluding article in this special issue is to examine whether the developmental courses for National Identification, in-group/out-group attitudes, and the relations between both variables could be characterized by general developmental patterns across different national settings. For this purpose the data from all participants in eight national studies were combined ($N = 725$) and subjected to the same sequence of analyses reported in the individual studies, be it that the most important independent variable now consisted of 12 levels representing the different national settings. The analyses revealed that the presence versus the absence of actual or recent armed conflict is the most important differentiating variable characterizing the national groups that participated in this study. Universal developmental courses for National Identification and in-group/out-group attitudes predicted by traditional theoretical models such as the CDT and SIDT cannot be maintained across different sociohistorical and political settings. The findings appear more consistent with theoretical models that incorporate reference to sociohistorical factors, such as the SSCMT and the IDCT.

Keywords: National identification; In-group/out-group attitudes; Cross-national; Comparative analyses; Intractable conflict.

INTRODUCTION

The purpose of this special issue was to report on the findings from eight studies dealing with National Identification and in-group/out-group attitudes with 7- and 11-year-old children from countries that have not

Correspondence should be addressed to Louis Oppenheimer, Department of Psychology, University of Amsterdam, Roetersstraat 15, NL-1018 WB Amsterdam, The Netherlands. E-mail: l.j.t.oppenheimer@uva.nl

© 2011 Psychology Press, an imprint of the Taylor & Francis Group, an Informa business
http://www.psypress.com/edp   DOI: 10.1080/17405629.2010.534277

experienced violence or war in the recent past (i.e., England and The Netherlands) and countries that have recently been or still are subject to armed conflict (i.e., Israel, Bosnia, north and south Cyprus, Northern Ireland, and the Basque Country).

In this article, the findings of the studies conducted in all of these countries are subjected to a cross-national comparative study. The major purpose of these analyses is to see whether patterns can be observed in the developmental course of National Identification and in-group/out-group attitudes with 7- and 11-year-olds that mature in different sociohistorical and political settings.

The findings from the Netherlands have not been presented in this special issue since they were found to be very similar to the findings from England, and neither have the findings from Israel been presented in this special issue. In the following cross-national comparative analyses, however, the data from the Netherlands as well as Israel are included.[1]

More specifically, the analyses will focus upon the assumption from cognitive-developmental theory (CDT) that, irrespective of the specific national context in which children mature, in-group favouritism and out-group derogation will be at their maximum around the age of 6 followed by reductions in in-group favouritism and out-group prejudice at later ages (Aboud, 1988, 2005; Aboud & Amato, 2001). According to Doyle and Aboud (1995), the decrease in in-group favouritism following the age of 6 is a consequence of a progressive development of underlying social-cognitive understanding of large groups (e.g., national groups). That is, while at age 6 children will primarily assign positive traits to members of the in-group and negative traits to members of out-groups, at later ages in-groups become less positively and out-groups less negatively evaluated. Of interest with respect to the latter predicted developmental change in in-group/out-group attitudes is the finding by Barrett and colleagues that out-groups that are perceived as the traditional enemy "are often evaluated significantly less positively than other out-groups" (Barrett, 2007, p. 268). In the presented series of studies, an out-group that is traditionally perceived as an enemy and at least one other neutral out-group were present.

In addition, in-group favouritism and out-group prejudice have been thought to be consequences of the extent of identification with the in-group or social group membership (Bigler, Brown, & Markell, 2001; Bigler & Liben, 2007). According to Barrett (2007; see also Barrett & Oppenheimer, 2011 this issue), this prediction implies that the extent of in-group favouritism and out-group prejudice should correlate positively with the

---

[1]The Israeli data were collected by Nadira Younis and Gabi Salomon (Haifa University, Israel). The data from the Netherlands were collected by Emina Midzic and Louis Oppenheimer.

strength of in-group identification. Furthermore, according to social identity development theory (SIDT; Nesdale, 1999), "the transition from mere in-group preference to out-group prejudice is facilitated when members are highly identified with a social group, and/or the in-group perceives a threat from an ethnic out-group" (Nesdale, Durkin, Maass, & Griffiths, 2005, p. 194). Whereas Nesdale et al. (2005; Nesdale, Maass, Griffiths, & Durkin, 2003) studied these processes using experimental minimal group paradigms, the data from the present studies involve national contexts in which real-life threatening out-groups have been and still are present. The findings of the present studies will be analysed to see whether the assumption derived from SIDT is valid over different sociohistorical and political settings.

Furthermore, it will be very interesting to examine whether the pattern of findings offers any information about the nature of the conflict in those sociohistorical settings that are characterized by recent or actual conflict, violence or war (i.e., Bosnia, Northern Ireland, Cyprus, Israel, and the Basque Country). In the integrative developmental-contextual theory (IDCT; Teichman & Bar-Tal, 2008) it is assumed that when "conflicts last for at least one generation, usually accompanied by various degrees of violence" and for which no immediate resolution is apparent, such conflicts can be characterized as intractable conflicts (see also Bar-On, 2006). When conflicts have become intractable, shared psychological intergroup repertoires (SPIRs) may have developed in these settings. According to Teichman and Bar-Tal (2008), a SPIR can be perceived as a "central socio-psychological infrastructure ... [that involves] ... narratives, beliefs, attitudes and emotions related to the causes of the conflict ... its course, goals, and solutions" (Teichman & Bar-Tal, 2008, p. 453). In other words, when the strength of National Identification or in-group/out-group attitudes with young children are extreme they may be assumed to be components of a SPIR and, hence, indicators of tractable or intractable conflicts (Bar-Tal, 2010; Bar-Tal & Teichman, 2005; Teichman & Bar-Tal, 2008). Within settings of intractable conflict, it is expected that for both parties in the conflict the attitudes towards the traditional enemy out-group should be (extremely) negative, while the in-group attitudes should be positive.

Finally, we will study the assumption that National Identification and its separate dimensions (i.e., degree, affect, negative and positive internalization, importance, and pride) are differentially affected by the national or political position of national, ethnic, and religious population groups involved in the present studies and the age of the children. Based on earlier research (Barrett, 2007; Barrett, Wilson, & Lyons, 2003) it is expected that the strength and importance of National Identification will increase between the ages of 7 and 11 years. Also with respect to this prediction, it is anticipated that the role of sociohistorical and political settings may play a modifying role (see the SSCMT model; Barrett, 2007; Barrett & Oppenheimer, 2011 this issue).

METHOD

Participants

In the present analyses, the data from 725 children aged 7 ($M = 7.17$; $SD = 0.49$; $n = 336$) and 11 years ($M = 11.02$; $SD = 0.50$; $n = 389$) were used. The children were derived from 12 national, ethnic, or religious settings consisting of England ($n = 80$), The Netherlands ($n = 82$), North Cyprus Turkish ($n = 71$), South Cyprus Greek ($n = 75$), Bosnia Bosniak ($n = 49$), Bosnia Serbian ($n = 40$), Israel Jewish ($n = 45$), Israel Arab ($n = 49$), Northern Ireland Catholic ($n = 69$), Northern Ireland Protestant ($n = 64$), Basque Country Basque ($n = 46$), and Basque Country Basque-Spanish ($n = 55$).

Because gender was not divided equally among the national groups and age groups and was not found to play a significant role in many of the preceding studies, gender was not included in the analyses. In addition, because Reizábal and Ortiz (this volume) used two traditional enemy out-groups for the Basque as well as the Basque-Spanish participants in their study, the attitudes towards both out-groups were averaged. First the results from the comparative analyses for National Identification are presented, followed by the results for the in-group/out-group attitudes, and finally, the relationships between these variables.

Materials

The data in the comparative analyses are based on the shared methodology in all the studies, involving the Strength of Identification Scale (SoIS; Barrett, 2007) and a trait attribution task (Barrett et al., 1997) by which in-group/out-group attitudes were assessed. For full details of all three tasks and the randomization procedures that were employed in their administration, see Barrett and Oppenheimer (2011 this issue).

RESULTS

National Identification

The first analysis dealt with the factor structure and reliability of the scale for National Identification. While a principal component analysis (*Determinant* = .362; *KMO* = .749; $\chi^2 = 622.78$, $df = 15$, $p < .001$) revealed a one-factor structure explaining 41.2% of the variance (*Eigenvalue* = 2.47), the Cronbach alpha for the scale attained .70. In Figure 1, the factor loadings (bold), average scores, and intercorrelations (italics) are schematically represented.

These findings allowed the computation of an average score for general National Identification (see also Table 1). A 12 × 2 (National Group ×

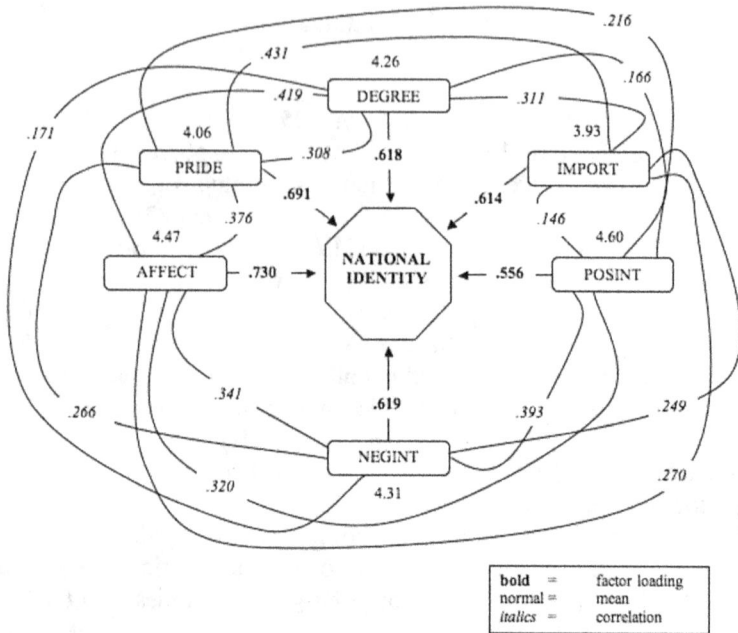

Figure 1. A schematic representation of the one-factor structure of National Identification, showing the factor loadings for (**bold**), the mean scores of (normal), and the correlations (*italics*) among the dimensions of National Identification for all participants combined.

Age) multivariate analysis of variance (MANOVA) on the average scores revealed a significant effect for the interaction, $F(11, 593) = 2.54, p < .01$, as well as for the main effects of Nation, $F(11, 593) = 22.20, p < .001$, and Age, $F(11, 593) = 9.88, p < .01$.

The findings show the highest National Identification to be present for the Bosnia-Serbian participants (i.e., 4.82) and the lowest for the Dutch and Basque-Spanish participants from the Basque country (i.e., 3.83 and 3.84, respectively).

With respect to age, the younger participants show a significantly higher level of National Identification (i.e., 4.33) than the older participants (i.e., 4.20).

However, because the one-structure model for National Identification fell apart in different sociohistorical and political settings, in the present analyses we focused on the separate dimensions of National Identification (i.e., degree, affect, negative and positive internalization, importance, and pride).

A 12 × 2 (National Group × Age) MANOVA on the mean scores of the six dimensions of National Identification (see Table 2) revealed significant

TABLE 1
The average mean scores ordered by size (and standard deviations) for general
National Identification for each national setting and age group as well as the outcomes
of post hoc pairwise Tukey's *t*-test comparisons among the national settings (e.g., the
difference between the Israeli Jewish participants [4] and the Dutch [1] and Basque
Country Basque-Spanish participants [2] is significant for both comparisons on the .05
level)

		Age			
	National group	*7*	*11*	*Total*	*Tukey*
[1]	Netherlands	4.04 (0.41)	3.60 (0.66)	**3.83** (0.58)	
[2]	Basque-Spanish	4.08 (0.30)	3.59 (0.39)	**3.84** (0.42)	
[3]	N. Ireland Protestant	4.06 (0.52)	3.96 (0.70)	**3.99** (0.63)	
[4]	Israel Jewish	4.14 (0.45)	4.21 (0.54)	**4.18** (0.50)	1**,2**
[5]	England	4.42 (0.64)	4.10 (0.49)	**4.26** (0.59)	1,2
[6]	Cyprus Greek	4.32 (0.60)	4.31 (0.60)	**4.32** (0.59)	1,2,3**
[7]	N. Ireland Catholic	4.44 (0.47)	4.34 (0.48)	**4.39** (0.47)	1,2,3
[8]	Cyprus Turkish	4.36 (0.53)	4.43 (0.52)	**4.39** (0.52)	1,2,3
[9]	Basque	4.31 (0.32)	4.45 (0.33)	**4.40** (0.32)	1,2,3*
[10]	Bosnia-Bosniak	4.63 (0.34)	4.41 (0.51)	**4.52** (0.45)	1,2,3,4**
[11]	Israel Arab	4.64 (0.31)	4.49 (0.51)	**4.56** (0.42)	1,2,3,4**,5**,6**
[12]	Bosnia-Serbian	4.76 (0.30)	4.86 (0.18)	**4.82** (0.24)	1,2,3,4,5,6,7*,8*,9*
	Age Average	4.33 (0.51)	4.20 (0.62)		

Note: Tukey's *t*-tests: $p \leq .001$; $*p < .01$; $**p < .05$.

National Group by Age interaction effects for negative internalization of,
$F(11, 593) = 2.62$, $p < .01$, and pride in, $F(11, 593) = 2.65$, $p < .01$ (see
Figure 2), the own nationality.

Significant main effects for Age were observed for degree of, $F(1,
593) = 6.72$, $p < .05$, affect towards, $F(1, 593) = 5.96$, $p < .05$, negative
internalization of, $F(1, 593) = 10.43$, $p = .001$, and importance of National
Identification, $F(1, 593) = 3.81$, $p = .05$. The main effect for Nation was
significant for all dimensions of National Identification with $F(11, 593)$-
values ranging from 5.25 for positive internalization to 15.39 for importance
of National Identification (for all effects $p < .001$).

These findings indicate that National Identification and the six
dimensions of National Identification are differentially related to the
sociohistorical and political setting in which they are assessed as well as
age. Large national, ethnic, and religious differences are present in the
degree of general National Identification.

In addition, while in some settings National Identification decreases
across age (e.g., with the Dutch, English, and Basque-Spanish participants),
in other settings no clear age-related changes were evident, while with
the Basque participants National Identification increases across age.

TABLE 2

Means (and standard deviations) for the six dimensions of National Identification for each national group (**bold**) and age group

NI-aspects	Netherlands			Cyprus Turkish			Cyprus Greek			Israel Jewish			Israel Arab			England		
	7	11	All	7	11	All	7	11	All	7	11	All	7	11	All	7	11	All
Degree	4.49 (0.83)	3.89 (0.99)	**4.21 (0.95)**	4.29 (1.14)	4.66 (0.70)	**4.46 (0.97)**	4.28 (1.02)	4.13 (1.04)	**4.17 (1.03)**	3.72 (0.66)	3.71 (0.99)	**3.71 (0.85)**	5.00 (0.00)	4.63 (0.63)	**4.82 (0.47)**	4.66 (0.87)	3.97 (0.63)	**4.38 (0.85)**
Affect	4.12 (0.54)	4.00 (0.79)	**4.06 (0.67)**	4.62 (0.85)	4.46 (0.69)	**4.55 (0.78)**	4.46 (1.05)	4.41 (0.80)	**4.42 (0.86)**	4.00 (0.58)	4.12 (0.81)	**4.10 (0.71)**	4.92 (0.28)	4.65 (0.71)	**4.79 (0.55)**	4.54 (0.84)	4.26 (0.73)	**4.43 (0.80)**
NegInt	3.79 (0.64)	3.41 (0.50)	**3.61 (0.60)**	4.12 (1.07)	4.36 (0.87)	**4.23 (0.98)**	4.69 (0.63)	4.35 (0.86)	**4.49 (0.82)**	4.31 (0.75)	4.59 (0.71)	**4.47 (0.73)**	4.88 (0.45)	4.39 (0.84)	**4.63 (0.71)**	4.54 (0.96)	4.05 (0.71)	**4.34 (0.89)**
PosInt	4.37 (0.49)	4.23 (0.74)	**4.31 (0.62)**	4.56 (0.56)	4.75 (0.44)	**4.65 (0.52)**	4.69 (0.63)	4.70 (0.76)	**4.69 (0.73)**	4.23 (0.60)	4.59 (0.62)	**4.43 (0.63)**	4.88 (0.34)	4.70 (0.88)	**4.79 (0.66)**	4.75 (0.52)	4.74 (0.45)	**4.75 (0.49)**
Importance	3.47 (1.05)	3.04 (1.19)	**3.27 (1.13)**	4.36 (1.20)	4.27 (0.92)	**4.32 (1.08)**	4.06 (1.48)	4.20 (1.15)	**4.17 (1.22)**	4.79 (0.53)	4.51 (0.69)	**4.63 (0.63)**	4.44 (1.10)	4.34 (0.81)	**4.39 (0.96)**	3.56 (1.44)	4.30 (0.95)	**3.46 (1.26)**
Pride	4.00 (0.93)	3.02 (1.45)	**3.52 (1.29)**	4.44 (0.99)	4.47 (1.05)	**4.46 (1.01)**	4.48 (1.17)	4.05 (1.20)	**4.14 (1.19)**	4.35 (0.73)	4.52 (0.82)	**4.45 (0.77)**	3.84 (1.17)	4.23 (0.89)	**4.03 (1.05)**	4.20 (1.36)	3.86 (1.01)	**4.06 (1.23)**

(continued).

TABLE 2
(Continued).

NI-aspects	Bosnia Bosniak			Bosnia Serbian			Northern Ireland Catholic			Northern Ireland Protestant			Basque Country Basque			Basque Country Basque-Spanish		
	7	11	All	7	11	All	7	11	All	7	11	All	7	11	All	7	11	All
Degree	4.81 (0.63)	4.26 (0.87)	**4.51 (0.81)**	4.83 (0.48)	4.80 (0.50)	**4.81 (0.49)**	4.19 (1.56)	4.00 (1.04)	**4.11 (1.35)**	3.58 (1.40)	3.67 (1.19)	**3.63 (1.25)**	4.63 (0.63)	4.77 (0.63)	**4.71 (0.62)**	3.93 (0.71)	3.47 (0.58)	**3.70 (0.68)**
Affect	4.67 (0.58)	4.62 (0.64)	**4.64 (0.61)**	4.94 (0.25)	5.00 (0.00)	**4.97 (0.16)**	4.70 (0.68)	4.62 (0.57)	**4.66 (0.63)**	4.38 (0.72)	4.20 (0.89)	**4.26 (0.83)**	4.93 (0.25)	4.85 (0.36)	**4.88 (0.32)**	4.45 (0.64)	3.82 (0.53)	**4.14 (0.66)**
NegInt	4.43 (0.81)	4.23 (0.65)	**4.32 (0.73)**	4.50 (0.63)	4.91 (0.44)	**4.73 (0.56)**	4.76 (0.44)	4.15 (0.93)	**4.49 (0.75)**	4.63 (0.72)	4.30 (0.79)	**4.41 (0.78)**	4.50 (0.73)	4.52 (0.75)	**4.51 (0.73)**	4.39 (0.52)	3.76 (0.56)	**4.07 (0.62)**
PosInt	4.38 (0.92)	4.62 (0.50)	**4.51 (0.72)**	4.69 (0.48)	5.00 (0.00)	**4.86 (0.35)**	4.64 (0.49)	4.62 (0.57)	**4.63 (0.52)**	4.56 (0.51)	4.53 (0.57)	**4.54 (0.55)**	4.94 (0.25)	4.85 (0.44)	**4.88 (0.39)**	4.54 (0.87)	4.23 (0.60)	**4.39 (0.76)**
Importance	4.81 (0.63)	4.18 (1.19)	**4.46 (1.02)**	4.83 (0.48)	4.62 (0.84)	**4.71 (0.71)**	4.09 (1.10)	4.10 (0.85)	**4.09 (0.99)**	3.40 (1.09)	3.43 (0.83)	**3.42 (0.92)**	4.45 (0.64)	4.81 (0.45)	**4.68 (0.55)**	4.04 (0.75)	3.61 (1.01)	**3.83 (0.91)**
Pride	4.80 (0.50)	4.58 (0.75)	**4.68 (0.65)**	4.75 (0.72)	4.87 (0.42)	**4.82 (0.56)**	4.42 (0.88)	4.35 (0.71)	**4.39 (0.81)**	3.74 (1.01)	3.63 (1.26)	**3.67 (1.17)**	3.98 (1.38)	4.72 (0.53)	**4.44 (0.99)**	4.40 (0.55)	3.85 (0.69)	**4.13 (0.68)**

Note: PosInt = Positive Internalization; NegInt = Negative Internalization.

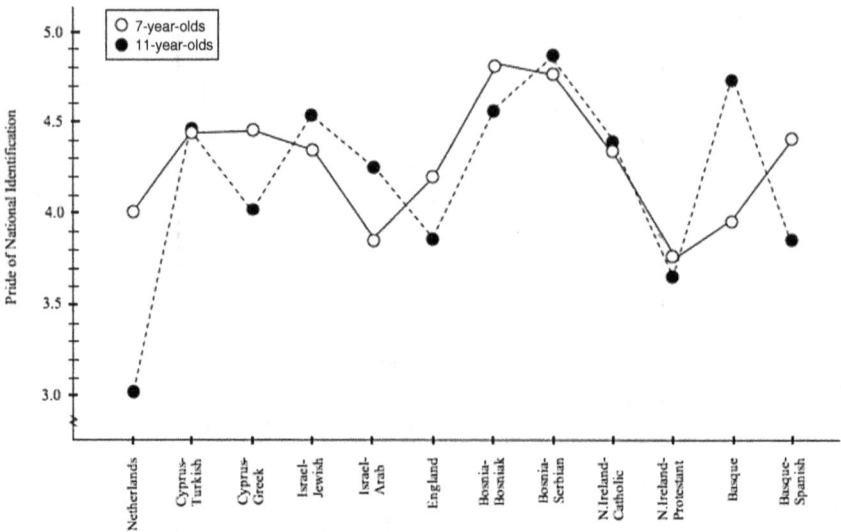

Figure 2. The graphic representation of the average scores for the separate dimension of pride of National Identification for each national group and age group.

The differential effects of national setting and age are more pronounced for the six separate dimensions of National Identification where effects of age were either absent or showed increases and decreases across age (see Figure 2, for the dimension of pride of National Identification).

In-group/out-group attitudes

Because in several studies, besides the traditional enemy out-group, only one neutral out-group was present, the analyses for in-group/out-group attitudes are conducted with respect to three groups only (i.e., the in-group, the traditional enemy out-group, and one neutral out-group).

A 12 × 2 (National Group × Age) MANOVA was conducted on the absolute scores for in-group and out-group evaluations (i.e., the positive minus the negative evaluations). This analysis revealed a significant interaction between National Group and Age for the evaluations of the in-group only, $F(11, 682) = 2.48$, $p < .01$. No significant effects for Age were present. For National Group, significant effects were evident with in-group, $F(11, 593) = 6.63$, $p < .001$, traditional enemy out-group, $F(11, 593) = 21.99$, $p < .001$, and neutral out-group evaluations, $F(11, 593) = 2.81$, $p = .001$. To best illustrate these significant effects for National Group, the average scores for in-group/out-group attitudes are schematically represented in Figure 3.

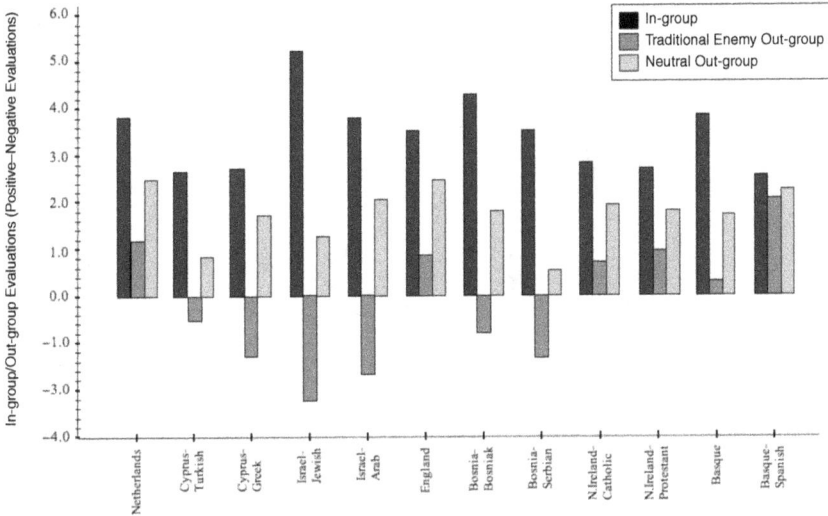

Figure 3. A schematic representation of the evaluations for the in-group, the traditional enemy out-group, and the neutral out-group for each national group.

The significant National Group by Age interaction demonstrated that, whereas for some national groups in-group evaluations decreased (i.e., The Netherlands, Cyprus Greek, Israel Jewish, and Bosnia Bosniak), other national groups did not show any significant change (e.g., England, Northern Ireland Catholic, and Basque-Spanish), while with others again increases in in-group evaluations were observed across age (e.g., Cyprus Turkish, Israel Arab, Bosnia Serbian, Northern Ireland Protestant, and Basque; see Figure 4).

The graph in Figure 4 also illustrates the significant differences in in-group evaluations across the different national groups. In addition, paired comparisons of the different evaluations showed in-group evaluations (i.e., 3.38) to be significantly higher than the evaluations of the neutral out-group (i.e., 1.64), $t(705) = 14.00$, $p < .001$, and the traditional enemy out-group (i.e., -0.04), $t(705) = 22.73$, $p < .001$. Also the evaluations of the neutral out-group differed significantly from those of the traditional enemy out-group, $t(705) = -12.51$, $p < .001$.

National Identification and in-group/out-group attitudes

The final set of analyses concerned the interrelationships among dimensions of National Identification and in-group/out-group attitudes. The inter-correlations among the variables are shown in Table 3. As can be observed from the table, while all dimensions of National Identification related

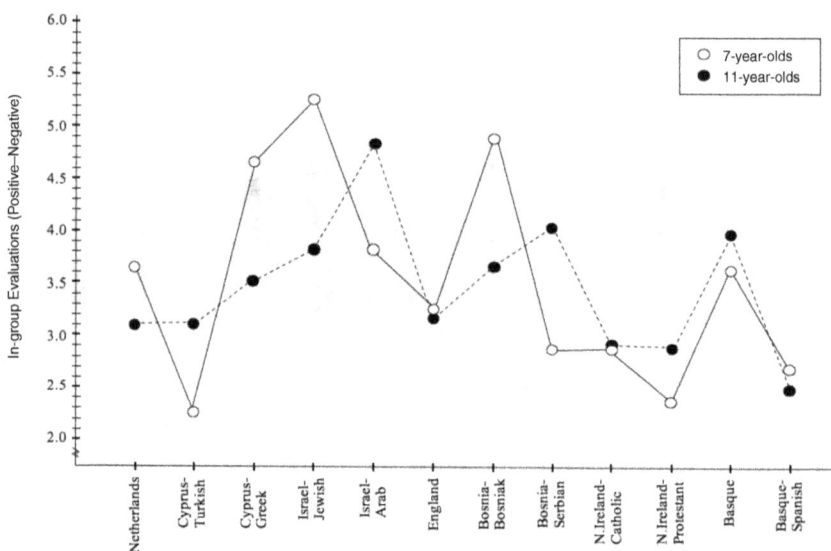

Figure 4. The graphic representation of the average scores for in-group evaluations for each national group and age group.

TABLE 3

The intercorrelations among the dimensions of National Identification (including the general score of National Identification; NatIdent) and the in-group/out-group attitudes

	Dimensions of National Identification						
Evaluations	Degree	Affect	NegInt	PosInt	Import	Pride	NatIdent
In-group	.077*	.080*	.123**	.138**	.142**	.172**	.188**
Enemy out-group	−.089*	−.115**	−.095*	−.038	−.189**	−.133**	−.174**
Neutral out-group	−.007	0.027	−.065	0.009	−.039	−.013	−.022

Note: *p < .05; **p < .01; PosInt = Positive Internalization; NegInt = Negative Internalization; NatIdent = General score for National Identification.

significantly positively or negatively to the evaluations of the in-group and the traditional enemy out-group, none of the dimensions related to the evaluations of the neutral out-group. Controlling for national group, age, and gender of the participants resulted only in marginal changes in the size of the relationships, but not in the pattern of relationships.

Of course, it should be taken into account that the significance of the rather weak correlations is primarily due to the large number of participants in these analyses (i.e., varying from 651 to 717). For that reason, stepwise regression analyses were conducted with the in-group and out-group evaluations as dependent variables and the dimensions of National

Identification as independent variables. These analyses revealed that in-group evaluations were primarily determined by the dimensions of pride and positive internalization of National Identification, $F(2, 648) = 13.84$, $p < .001$; with β-values of 0.15 ($t = 3.85$, $p < .001$) and 0.11 ($t = 2.79$, $p < .01$) for pride and positive internalization, respectively.

The evaluations of the traditional enemy out-group was determined by importance of National Identification only, $F(2, 649) = 24.01$, $p < .001$; with β-value -0.19 ($t = -4.90$, $p < .001$). None of the dimensions of National Identification played a role in the evaluations of the neutral out-group.

DISCUSSION AND CONCLUSION

The purpose of the comparative analyses was to examine cross-national patterns in the development of National Identification, in-group/out-group attitudes, and the relationships among National Identification and in-group/out-group attitudes. The most important differentiating variable character-izing the national groups that participated in the individual studies and the comparative analyses was the presence versus the absence of actual or recent armed conflict.

Because gender was not equally divided over the different national groups, gender was not included in the comparative analyses. For insights into the role of gender in National Identification, in-group/out-group attitudes, and the relationships among dimensions of National Identification and the evaluations, the reader should refer to the individual studies reported in this issue.

The sociohistorical and political settings from which the data on National Identification and its separate dimensions (i.e., degree, affect, negative and positive internalization, importance, and pride) were obtained had determin-ing effects on the strength and importance of National Identification in the different settings. The data did not permit any unequivocal conclusion with respect to changes in *general* National Identification across age. When the data from all national, ethnic, and religious groups were averaged, the younger participants showed a higher strength of National Identification than the older participants. This finding runs counter to our expectation that the strength and importance of National Identification would increase between the ages of 7 and 11 years (Barrett, 2007; Barrett et al., 2003).

However, this undifferentiated finding is immediately modified when the different national groups are taken into account. Then in some settings National Identification decreases from 7 to 11 years, in other settings increases are observed, while in most settings no clear changes are present.

The same finding holds for the separate dimensions of National Identification. In particular with respect to pride of National Identification and negative internalization (i.e., the extent to which the participants were troubled by negative opinions about their country by others) the effects of national setting and age were most pronounced. For instance, the strength of pride of National Identification decreased for the Dutch, Cyprus-Greek, English, and Basque-Spanish participants, increased for the Israel-Arab and Basque participants, and remained unchanged for the remainder (i.e., for the Cyprus-Turkish, Israel-Jewish, Bosnia-Bosniak, Bosnia-Serbian, Northern Ireland-Catholic, and Northern Ireland-Protestant participants). The patterns observed for the six aspects of National Identification are different in and affected by the sociohistorical and political backgrounds of the participants in the various studies. Hence, the patterns, nature, and strength for the six dimensions of National Identification represent context-, age-, and gender-dependent constructs that make any generalization of this construct within and across national, ethnic, and religious settings extremely problematic.

The findings for in-group/out-group attitudes (i.e., attitudes) support the earlier conclusion with respect to National Identification. The findings only partially support the assumption derived from CDT that irrespective of the specific national context a reduction in in-group favouritism and out-group derogation will be evident from the age of 6 (Aboud, 1988, 2005; Aboud & Amato, 2001). This assumption implies that while at age 7 children will primarily assign positive traits to members of the in-group and negative characteristics to members of out-groups, at later ages in-groups become less positively and out-groups less negatively evaluated. This was found for some particular sociohistorical and political settings only (i.e., the Dutch, Cyprus-Greek, Israel-Jewish, and Bosnia-Bosniak national groups). However, for the English, Northern Ireland-Catholic, Basque, and Basque-Spanish national groups no changes were evident, while for the Cyprus-Turkish, Israel-Arab, Bosnia-Serbian, and Northern Ireland-Protestant national groups clear increases in positive evaluations of the in-group were observed from age 7 to age 11. In other words, the perception of the in-group and its evaluation is very much dependent on the sociohistorical setting and apparently also on the position of the national group in a particular setting. It can be argued that the increase in positive evaluations of the in-group across age is the result of a greater awareness (i.e., knowledge acquisition) of the position of a particular national, ethnic, or religious group (i.e., as minority group) within a larger political setting. In addition, the struggle of some of these in-groups towards a larger level of autonomy or independence may also play a role in the higher positive evaluations of the in-group. These questions definitely require more study.

In the present analysis of the data, we focused on the absolute in-group/out-group attitudes by subtracting the negative from the positive scores. The findings with regard to the evaluations of the in-group, traditional enemy out-group, and a neutral out-group were schematically presented in Figure 3. The resulting graph can be read as a complex interaction involving historical and political variables such as the duration and severity of a conflict, the time that has elapsed between the conflict and the presence of, as well as opportunities for, contact between in-groups and (traditional enemy) out-groups. In addition, social and psychological variables may be involved dealing with the positivity of in-group evaluations (i.e., in-group esteem and derived individual self-esteem) and the way it affects out-group evaluations, as well as the role of education, the media, and collective memory (i.e., the societal attitude towards particular out-groups; see Barrett, 2007; Barrett & Oppenheimer, 2011 this issue).

Furthermore, the (extreme) negative attitudes towards enemy out-groups within settings of conflict (i.e., Israel, Bosnia, and Cyprus) may be evidence for the presence of shared psychological intergroup repertoires (SPIRs; Teichman & Bar-Tal, 2008) within different national groups that are the result of intractable conflicts. Whereas Teichman and Bar-Tal (2008) define intractable conflicts as "conflicts between political, cultural, or ethnic groups ... that last at least 25 years ... and evolve over goals that are perceived as existential, unsolvable, and of zero sum nature" (p. 453), the present data suggest that some of these conflicts are not intractable (e.g., Northern Ireland and the Basque Country) whereas others (still) are (e.g., Israel, Bosnia, and Cyprus). It can be argued that the presence of (extreme) negative attitudes, stereotypes, and/or prejudice with 7- and 11-year-old children may be the result of SPIRs that can only develop in societies involved in an intractable conflict (e.g., Israel; Bar-Tal & Teichman, 2005). According to Bar-Tal (2010), collective memories form one of the three elements of the infrastructure in intractable conflicts. Collective memories may then become a remnant, though persistent, of past severe or intractable conflicts (Oppenheimer & Hakvoort, 2003).

For instance, the two national settings that have not experienced violence or war in the recent past are England and The Netherlands. While for both countries more than 60 years have passed since the Second World War, the traditional enemy out-group (for both countries, Germany) is very differently evaluated compared to a neutral out-group (for both countries, France). Despite the years that have passed since the Second World War, the Dutch and the English participants evaluated France significantly more positively than Germany. This is not surprising since, until recently, studies in the Netherlands have suggested that Germany is still perceived as the traditional enemy out-group and is more negatively evaluated than other countries in Europe (Dekker, Aspeslagh, & Winkel, 1997; Jansen, 1993; Oppenheimer & Hakvoort, 2003; Peters, 1998; Peters & Schuyt, 1998). The present findings show that with respect to the effects of the Second World War, as maintained in collective memories, even 60 years are not sufficient for changes in the evaluation of a "traditional enemy" out-group to occur.

In the Basque Country, the Basque national group clearly evaluates the traditional enemy groups (i.e., Spain and France) less positively than the in-group and the neutral out-group (Italy), though still positively. The Basque-Spanish national group demonstrated a more egalitarian perception of out-groups since no differences are present in the evaluations of the in-group, traditional enemy out-groups, and the neutral out-group. All groups are equally, positively evaluated.

The Northern Ireland Catholic and Protestant religious groups are almost identical in their evaluations of themselves (i.e., in-group), the traditional enemy out-groups (i.e., the Protestants and Catholics, respectively), and the neutral out-group (i.e., Scotland). While the neutral out-group is less positively evaluated than the in-group, the traditional enemy groups are again less positively evaluated than the neutral out-group. Apparently, more time is required to result in more positive evaluations of the traditional enemy out-groups and reconciliation.

The findings from Cyprus, Bosnia-Herzegovina and Israel show the effects from more recent and present armed conflicts. Apparently, the more recent the conflict, the more negative the traditional enemy out-group is evaluated, a finding that is well illustrated by the still present Israeli–Palestinian conflict and the extreme negative evaluations of the traditional enemy out-groups. Again, time in combination with the type of resolution of the conflict may be the determining factors resulting in changes in the attitudes of (former) enemies towards each other.

With the exception of the Basque-Spanish participants, the findings from the in-group/out-group attitudes support Barrett's (2007) argument that traditional enemy out-groups are evaluated less positively than neutral out-groups.

In the literature on in-group/out-group attitudes, it is often assumed that the extent of positive in-group evaluations and out-group derogation will relate to the strength of National Identification. The findings of the present comparative analyses do not offer strong support for this assumption. No evidence was found for an association between the six dimensions of National Identification and the evaluations of neutral out-groups. The extent to which the in-group is evaluated positively (i.e., in-group esteem) seems to be affected by pride in National Identification and the importance individuals attach to positive comments about their own national group. The extent to which the traditional enemy out-group is less positively or even negatively evaluated relates to the importance attached to being a member of a particular in-group and the extent to which individuals are troubled by negative comments about their own in-group. However, it is not clear whether these dimensions are the cause for the strength of in-group and out-group evaluations. It may be possible that a reversed causal relationship is present and that the level of in-group esteem and derived self-esteem determine feelings of pride and good feelings about positive comments about the in-group and that less positive and negative attitudes towards the traditional enemy out-group result in the perception of the in-group as important and the experience of bad feelings about negative comments about the in-group. Additional research is necessary to detail the exact nature of these relationships.

The latter line of reasoning might also function as an explanatory argument for the diversity in the findings with respect to the dimensions of National Identification across the different national groups. Depending on the position of each group within a particular national setting (e.g., majority vs. minority; with or without a striving towards larger autonomy or independence; and so on), different aspects of National Identification may be affected and (de)emphasized.

In short, the findings from the individual studies as well as the comparative analyses show that theoretical models such as CDT and SIDT that predict universal (developmental) courses for National Identification and in-group/out-group attitudes cannot be maintained across different sociohistorical and political settings. Whereas common patterns appear to exist depending on the severity and duration of, and time elapsed between, an armed conflict and the present, each national setting is also characterized by its own pattern of changes in National Identification and in-group/out-group attitudes across time (i.e., age), that do not confirm to the predictions of either CDT or SIDT. Instead, theories that explicitly incorporate reference to sociohistorical factors, such as the SSCMT (Barrett, 2007; see Barrett & Oppenheimer, 2011 this issue) and the IDCT (Teichman & Bar-Tal, 2008), would appear to be more consistent with the evidence from the current sequence of studies.

REFERENCES

Aboud, F. E. (1988). *Children and prejudice*. Oxford, UK: Blackwell.

Aboud, F. E. (2005). The development of prejudice in childhood and adolescence. In J. F. Dovidio, P. Glick, & L. A. Budman (Eds.), *On the nature of prejudice: Fifty years after Allport* (pp. 311–326). Oxford, UK: Blackwell.

Aboud, F. E., & Amato, M. (2001). Developmental and socialization influences on intergroup bias. In R. Brown & S. L. Gaertner (Eds.), *Blackwell handbook of social psychology: Intergroup processes* (pp. 65–85). Oxford, UK: Blackwell.

Bar-On, D. (2006). Stereotypes and prejudice in conflict: Representations of Arabs in Israeli-Jewish society [Review]. *Israel Studies, 11*(2), 75–80.

Barrett, M. (2007). *Children's knowledge, beliefs and feelings about nations and national groups.* Hove, UK: Psychology Press.

Barrett, M., Lyons, E., Bennett, M., Vila, I., Giménez, A., Arcuri, L., et al. (1997). *Children's beliefs and feelings about their own and other national groups in Europe.* Final Report to the Commission of the European Communities, Directorate-General XII for Science, Research and Development, Human Capital and Mobility (HCM) Programme, Research Network Contract No. CHRX-CT94-0687.

Barrett, M., & Oppenheimer, L. (2011). Findings, theories and methods in the study of children's national identifications and national attitudes. *European Journal of Developmental Psychology, 8,* 5–24.

Barrett, M., Wilson, H., & Lyons, E. (2003). The development of national in-group bias: English children's attributions of characteristics to English, American and German people. *British Journal of Developmental Psychology, 21,* 193–220.

Bar-Tal, D. (2010). Culture of conflict: Evolvement, institutionalization, and consequences. In R. Schwarzer & P. A. French (Eds.), *Personality, human development, and culture: International perspectives on psychological science* (Vol. 2, pp. 183–198). Hove, UK: Psychology Press.

Bar-Tal, D., & Teichman, Y. (2005). *Stereotypes and prejudice in conflict: Representations of Arabs in Israeli-Jewish society.* Cambridge, UK: Cambridge University Press.

Bigler, R. S., Brown, C., & Markell, M. (2001). When groups are not created equal: Effects of group status on the formation of intergroup attitudes in children. *Child Development, 72,* 1151–1162.

Bigler, R. S., & Liben, L. S. (2007). Developmental intergroup theory: Explaining and reducing children's social stereotyping and prejudice. *Current Directions in Psychological Science, 16,* 162–166.

Dekker, H., Aspeslagh, R., & Winkel, B. (1997). *Burenverdriet: Attituden ten aanzien van de lidstaten van de Europese Unie* [Neighbour sorrow: Attitudes towards the member states of the European Union]. Den Haag, The Netherlands: Clingendael.

Doyle, A. B., & Aboud, F. E. (1995). A longitudinal study of White children's racial prejudice as a social-cognitive development. *Merrill-Palmer Quarterly, 41,* 209–228.

Jansen, L. B. (1993). *Bekend en onbemind: Het beeld van Duitsland en Duitsers onder jongeren van vijftien tot negentien jaar* [Known and unloved: The image of Germany and Germans among youth aged 15 to 19 years]. Den Haag, The Netherlands: Clingendael.

Nesdale, D. (1999). Social identity and ethnic prejudice in children. In P. Martin & W. Noble (Eds.), *Psychology and society* (pp. 92–110). Brisbane, Australia: Australian Academic Press.

Nesdale, D., Durkin, K., Maass, A., & Griffiths, J. (2005). Threat, group identification, and children's ethnic prejudice. *Social Development, 14,* 189–205.

Nesdale, D., Maass, A., Griffiths, J., & Durkin, K. (2003). Effects of in-group and out-group ethnicity on children's attitudes towards members of the in-group and out-group. *British Journal of Developmental Psychology, 21,* 177–192.

Oppenheimer, L., & Hakvoort, I. (2003). Will the Germans ever be forgiven? Memories of the Second World War generations later. In E. Cairns & M. D. Roe (Eds.), *The role of memory in ethnic conflict* (pp. 94–104). Basingstoke, UK: Palgrave-Macmillan.

Peters, S. (1998). Mythische waas rond oorlog moet verdwijnen [Mythical air surrounding the war has to disappear]. *Historisch Nieuwsblad* [Historical Newsletter], 7(3), 18–23.

Peters, S., & Schuyt, M. (1998). Weinig kennis, veel moralisme [Little knowledge, much moralism]. *Historisch Nieuwsblad, 7*(3), 24–27.

Teichman, Y., & Bar-Tal, D. (2008). Acquisition and development of a shared psychological intergroup repertoire in a context of intractable conflict. In S. M. Quintana & C. McKown (Eds.), *Handbook of race, racism, and the developing child* (pp. 452–482). Hoboken, NJ: Wiley.

For Product Safety Concerns and Information please contact our EU
representative GPSR@taylorandfrancis.com
Taylor & Francis Verlag GmbH, Kaufingerstraße 24, 80331 München, Germany

www.ingramcontent.com/pod-product-compliance
Lightning Source LLC
Chambersburg PA
CBHW050534270326
41926CB00015B/3219